TO THE READER

Dianetics (from Greek *dia* "through," and *nous* "soul") delineates fundamental principles of the mind and spirit. Through the application of these discoveries, it became apparent that Dianetics dealt with a beingness that defied time—the human spirit—originally denominated the "I" and subsequently the "thetan." From there, Mr. Hubbard continued his research, eventually mapping the path to full spiritual freedom for the individual.

Dianetics is a forerunner and substudy of Scientology which, as practiced by the Church, addresses only the "thetan" (spirit), which is senior to the body, and its relationship to and effects on the body.

This book is presented in its original form and is part of L. Ron Hubbard's religious literature and works and is not a statement of claims made by the author, publisher or any Church of Scientology. It is a record of Mr. Hubbard's observations and research into life and the nature of man.

Neither Dianetics nor Scientology is offered as, nor professes to be physical healing, nor is any claim made to that effect. The Church does not accept individuals who desire treatment of physical or mental illness but, instead, requires a competent medical examination for physical conditions, by qualified specialists, before addressing their spiritual cause.

The Hubbard® Electrometer, or E-Meter, is a religious artifact used in the Church. The E-Meter, by itself, does nothing and is only used by ministers and ministers-in-training, qualified in its use, to help parishioners locate the source of spiritual travail.

The attainment of the benefits and goals of Dianetics and Scientology requires each individual's dedicated participation, as only through one's own efforts can they be achieved.

We hope reading this book is the first step of a personal voyage of discovery into this new and vital world religion.

THIS BOOK BELONGS TO

Advanced PROCEDURE and AXIOMS

Advanced PROCEDURE and AXIOMS

L. RON HUBBARD

Bridge Publications, Inc.

A
HUBBARD®
Publication

BRIDGE PUBLICATIONS, INC.
4751 Fountain Avenue
Los Angeles, California 90029

ISBN 978-1-4031-4414-0

Printed in the United States of America

IMPORTANT NOTE

In reading this book, be very certain you never go past a word you do not fully understand. The only reason a person gives up a study or becomes confused or unable to learn is because he or she has gone past a word that was not understood.

The confusion or inability to grasp or learn comes AFTER a word the person did not have defined and understood. It may not only be the new and unusual words you have to look up. Some commonly used words can often be misdefined and so cause confusion.

This datum about not going past an undefined word is the most important fact in the whole subject of study. Every subject you have taken up and abandoned had its words which you failed to get defined.

Therefore, in studying this book be very, very certain you never go past a word you do not fully understand. If the material becomes confusing or you can't seem to grasp it, there will be a word just earlier that you have not understood. Don't go any further, but go back to BEFORE you got into trouble, find the misunderstood word and get it defined.

GLOSSARIES

In writing *Advanced Procedure and Axioms*, L. Ron Hubbard provided a glossary of all technical terms, defined as they are used in this book and in the sequence they should be learned. As such, the *LRH Glossary* forms a vital component of this text to be studied in full for a thorough comprehension of the nomenclature and subject itself.

To further aid reader comprehension, LRH directed the editors to provide definitions for other words and phrases. These are included in the *Appendix, Editor's Glossary of Words, Terms and Phrases*. Words sometimes have several meanings. The *Editor's Glossary* only contains the definitions of words as they are used in this text. Other definitions can be found in standard language or Dianetics and Scientology dictionaries.

If you find any other words you do not know, look them up in a good dictionary.

Advanced Procedure and Axioms

$\mathcal{C}$ONTENTS

This is Advanced Procedure

This is Authorized Procedure

*I*NTRODUCTION

*I*NTRODUCTION

*T*HERE ARE THREE POINTS of address in any case. These are THOUGHT, EMOTION and EFFORT.

The use of these three is established by the estimation by the auditor of the preclear on the Tone Scale. In any relatively high-level case, all three may be used interchangeably.

There are five types of cases. The types are HIGH-TONE, NORMAL, NEUROTIC, DRAMATIZING PSYCHOTIC and COMPUTING PSYCHOTIC. These are bracketed successively from 5.0 down the scale to below 2.0.

There are two case aspects. These are WIDE-OPEN and OCCLUDED.

Every case has one or more COMPUTATIONS, one or more SERVICE FACSIMILES, one or more DRAMATIZATIONS, one or more SYMPATHY EXCITERS, one or more PRESENT TIME PROBLEMS, one or more FUTURE GOALS and only one EMOTIONAL CURVE since this is common to every case.

These data combine into any aspect of any case and solve any case.

An outline, definition and description of these data is the subject of this brief manual.

SELF-DETERMINISM

*"The extent of free choice
is remarkable."*

$\mathcal{S}$ELF-DETERMINISM

HE KEY TO the processes outlined in this book lies in the SELF-DETERMINISM of individuals.

Man has arrived at a place where he is capable of controlling his environment to an extent much greater than he has ever realized.

The results of self-determined action and the action itself may be modified by the environment which, by space, gravity and such matters, limits the action of the human being. *But* this does not alter the fact that the mind attempts full self-determinism and to a very marked extent achieves it.

Along each and every dynamic, the mind makes a self-determined effort. Self-determinism is positive and strong in its native state.

The only thing which can actually alter self-determinism and reduce it is self-determinism itself. One can determine to be used or worked upon by the environ and its people. But until one makes a determination to do so, one is not so affected.

Each and every aberration of the human mind and the human body has an initial postulate to be so aberrated. Engrams are effective only when the individual himself determines that they will be effective.

Every individual has what is called a SERVICE FACSIMILE.

This is actually part of a chain of incidents which the individual uses to invite sympathy or cooperation on the part of the environment. One uses engrams to handle himself and others and the environ after one has himself conceived that he has failed to handle himself, others and the general environ.

At first an individual is completely aware that he is using engrams. Then the use of them, itself, becomes a curtain to that awareness and proceeds toward an automatic (but nonetheless self-determined) use of the engrams.

When one fails as himself, he explains that failure even to himself by *consciously,* at first, choosing his service facsimile. Thereafter, his own body and mental condition become subject to it.

The first self-determinism which leads to aberration is the decision "to be human." The affinity, reality and communication indulged in by a human being is necessary to being human. One determines to exert ARC. One then becomes subject to what he has determined. ARC with individuals in a very aberrated state is necessarily a very low ARC. It is not that ARC is bad, but that ARC with low-toned individuals is bad.

Any individual under processing can be discovered to be using service facsimiles. Everything which is wrong with him, he has selectively and particularly chosen to be wrong with him.

Every thought or computation has behind it a physical observation, or EFFORT or COUNTER-EFFORT.

But there is also a free source of theta which is, itself, continually self-determining or is capable of doing so. Thus it is not necessary to exhaust efforts and counter-efforts, since the individual has *free choice* in his use of those efforts or counter-efforts.

Every aberration, every service facsimile is non-survival. The individual evaluated a situation, found it necessary in order to go on living, in any case, to use a service facsimile. But the moment it was used, he became ever afterwards subject to it.

In such a wise, an individual became the effect of his own causes.

It is the role of the auditor to discover, with the preclear, the moments when the preclear postulated conclusions of any kind on any subject. These conclusions are occasionally smothered by mis-emotion, such as sympathy, and by general ARC. They can also be smothered by physical pain.

The running of engrams is itself a therapy. Self-determinism Processing and Emotion Processing are finer and more complete levels of processing, since they reach all cases which can be gotten into present time communication. The engram is *never* effective until the individual chooses to use it.

It is interesting that choosing to use an engram on any dynamic also includes, when the operation fails, all other dynamics. Thus any non-survival wish or action, *if it fails,* recoils upon the user. One postulates a non-survival action for a group or for another person or a life form and, *if it fails,* is subjected to it himself—again by his own choice! Thus trying to stop somebody from coughing by being annoyed will result, if the effort fails, in starting one coughing.

Here is a mechanism, interposed in the cycle of stimulus-response restimulation, which demonstrates that:

WHEREAS SURFACE OBSERVATION SAYS THAT RESTIMULATION CAN OCCUR, DEEPER STUDY SHOWS THAT AN INTERIM STEP OF SELF-DETERMINISM IS NECESSARY FOR *ANY* RESTIMULATION TO TAKE PLACE.

Man is so aberrated at this date that it took considerable processing to discover this interim factor. And to discover that the interim factor is far more important than the mechanism of restimulation and that restimulation ceases by picking up the inner postulate between a source of restimulation and being restimulated.

The extent of free choice is remarkable. The amount a case can be improved by Self-determinism Processing is even more remarkable.

It may be hard for one to realize, at first, that he wished himself ill. But recall the time when you tried to get out of school or work. In such a wise, one wished all his ailments upon himself.

There is also, with self-determinism, the emotion of *intention*. That emotion with which one enters an incident greatly influences the effort and can be run as emotion. Running "determinism" as an emotion, whether to see or to get rid of a psychosomatic illness, produces broad results. Run the emotion of "determinism" off a lifetime and one picks up all non-survival courses. The effort itself falls away, untouched but cancelled.

JUSTICE

*"Infinite rightness would be
infinite survival."*

*J*USTICE

HUMAN BEINGS HAVE a very high native sense of JUSTICE.

JUSTICE could be called the adjudication of the relative rightness or wrongness of a decision or an action. (See Logic 7.)

Infinite rightness would be infinite survival. How wrong can a person be? Dead!

When the individual is small, he cannot enforce justice except by using relatively low-scale ARC. Instead of forthright action, then, a thing which he will attempt but which will fail, he is capable of making the aberrated effort of gaining sympathy to prove his point.

All service facsimiles are used out of an effort to stay in ARC, however low-scale. The individual, failing in his childish lack of strength to effect justice when he has been wronged, retains the facsimile of the injustice and everything consequent upon it as living proof of the wrong which has been done him. Thus one finds AAs and birth rather commonly in restimulation, but only after they have been called into play by the individual himself. Men recover from injuries. But they do not recover, short of processing, from their own self-determinism.

The major service facsimile keys are, then, to be found in an area of injustice which is crass and blunt and which is very much in the awareness of the preclear. They occur, these key incidents, anytime from two to ten or even later. The individual answers the injustice by wishing off the injury or illness upon another. This failing, he takes it himself. Later sympathy for the purveyor of poor justice and general ARC self-determinism can occlude these service facsimiles of injustice.

The resolution of the service facsimile depends, then, upon getting up enough self-determined postulates and enough sympathy and other emotion to lay bare, in clarity, a part of the chain. Then one breaks up the chain.

The difference between Homo sapiens and Homo novis is that Homo sapiens is uniformly using a service facsimile or the whole chain and does not realize that he is using it, but explains it as disease or "mental illness" or "psychosomatic illness," while Homo novis is not using the service facsimile and knows what he can occasion with himself.

In relatively skilled hands, it is a twenty-five- to fifty-hour process to advance a Homo sapiens to a Homo novis. This compares to a two-hundred- to a two-thousand-hour process of running engrams. The engrams do not need to be run, but become ineffective when the determinism to have them is cleared away.

Justice and injustice should be kept in mind throughout the process.

THE ROLE
OF THE AUDITOR

*"An auditor is most successful when
he has achieved an inexorable self-confidence
in himself, in his tools, in his attitude
toward the preclear and in the results
he means and determines to achieve."*

$\mathcal{T}$HE ROLE OF THE AUDITOR

N AUDITOR IS essentially a technician.

Existing techniques are such as to determine a scathing fact:

AN AUDITOR WHO CANNOT ACHIEVE RESULTS DOES NOT KNOW HIS TOOLS.

Existing techniques are tools. Any tool requires intelligent handling and a deftness in application.

The user of any tool—whether it be a stone ax, an adz or a Geiger counter—must acquire confidence in that tool and confidence in his ability to use that tool.

An auditor is most successful when he has achieved an inexorable self-confidence in himself, in his tools, in his attitude toward the preclear and in the results he means and determines to achieve.

Any science is to some degree an art. The less variation in its results, the less it is an art. A perfect and "invariable" science still would contain the variable of its applicator. However, for the first time in the history of Man, we have achieved minimal variation of application. For we can restore the native ability of the individual applicator to be self-confident. There is no argument about the exactness of our processes.

Nothing, tritely and truly, succeeds like success in auditing. Restored confidence in self, aided by success in results, markedly shortens for the auditor the time he will have to spend on any preclear and increases his level of success.

An auditor should attain personal and general self-confidence. He should then attain a good theoretical knowledge of his tools. He should have a period of application wherein he gains an excellent practical knowledge of those tools. He should then have several signal successes. If these steps are followed, an auditor's use of his science should be certain and broad.

THE EVOLUTION OF A MAN

"The auditor is causing any preclear he processes to evolve into a higher plane than was hitherto reached on the evolutionary scale."

*T*HE EVOLUTION
OF A MAN

*M*AN EVIDENTLY BEGAN as a monocell, without intercellular relation problems.

He developed by counter-efforts to a degree which banded together many cells with one CENTRAL CONTROL CENTER.

He joined then with a SECOND CONTROL CENTER and, dual, evolved organically into Man.

The problems of the monocell by itself were strenuous but uncomplicated, having relationship only with the environment in its grossest form—pure MEST. These problems included such phenomena as the explosion of cosmic rays.

The problems of a cellular colony under one control center were yet similar to those of the monocell. The protagonist had but one personality and one antagonist—MEST. Vegetable and invertebrate problems are found in this period.

The problems of the dual-control stage began severely and continued in confusion.

Interpersonal relations, when in difficulty, have their root in the elementary problems of the dual-control problems—wherein the current control center confuses its ancient problems with its partner center, with the problems the organism may have with other individuals in the environment.

The evolution of Man presents many fascinating aspects, but they have basic simplicities. There are, essentially, only two sets of problems:

THE PROBLEMS BETWEEN THE CONTROL CENTER OF THE MIND AND THE ELEMENTS.

THE PROBLEM OF THE CONTROL CENTER OF THE MIND WITH ITS ALTERNATE CONTROL CENTER.

An auditor need resolve, in any case, the essential basic confusions of the preclear in each of these two sets.

The evolution of Man is to date organic. At this date we have introduced another evolution level—THOUGHT.

The auditor is causing any preclear he processes to evolve into a higher plane than was hitherto reached on the evolutionary scale. He is *not* re-establishing a past "norm." His goal is:

THE ESTABLISHMENT OF THE POTENTIAL CONTROL CENTER AS THE SELF-DETERMINED CENTER OF CONTROL OF THE MIND.

The work of the auditor is not related to any past -ology, but to evolution itself. It is not medical nor biological nor psychological, no matter if these enter incidentally as byproducts of processing. That which the auditor is doing has no past standards.

BUT IT HAS ITS OWN STANDARD, ITS OWN OPERATION, AS PRECISE AS BUILDING ANY BRIDGE.

The goal must not be violated or lessened.

ADVANCED PROCEDURE

*"The essence of Advanced Procedure
is to follow it step by step."*

ADVANCED PROCEDURE

*(Every technical term here is
defined in LRH Glossary.)*

HE AUDITOR AND PRECLEAR are a group.

To function well, a group must be cleared.

The clearing of a group is not difficult. It requires little time.

The relationship of the auditor and preclear is not parity. The auditor lends himself to the group as the control center of the group until the preclear, as sub-control center, is established under his own control center's command. The role of the auditor ceases at that moment.

The auditor necessarily owns the preclear. He owns the preclear on a lessening basis until the preclear owns himself.

If the auditor wishes to successfully *own,* to the end of *not* owning the preclear, he must not use the preclear to the service of the auditor. For this establishes and confirms the ownership and inhibits the preclear from owning himself.

The First Act of the auditor concerns HIMSELF. He assesses the task, rather than the preclear, and assesses the matter within himself. He establishes whether or not he desires the preclear to become established under the preclear's own center of control. To do this, the auditor may find it necessary to Straightwire himself for the removal of any reason why he does not want this preclear to be owned by the preclear. He then postulates, to himself, what he wants to happen with this preclear and postulates, as well, that he can do his task with this preclear. He must feel these postulates solidly. If he cannot, he must discover why he cannot. Thus the first session's first minutes with the preclear are concerned with the auditor himself. He should take time out from the preclear until he, himself, is established in his task and then readdress the preclear.

The Second Act in addressing the PRECLEAR is to clear the preclear of PAST POSTULATES which may have concerned someone with whom the preclear may have the auditor confused.

The Third Act consists of cleaning PRESENT TIME FACSIMILES for the preclear so that the environment is not confused.

The Fourth Act is establishing ACCESSIBILITY of the preclear with himself. This may include a thorough address to past auditing and auditors.

No further action than these can be successfully accomplished until these have been accomplished.

In the case of psychotics, the Second, Third and Fourth Acts may be changed in their order, but they are vital. They are so thoroughly vital that one might say that a psychotic case, computing or dramatizing, will be "broken" only by following out these four Acts and, conversely, that the use of these four Acts will themselves break a psychotic case.

Until these four Acts are accomplished (and they must be accomplished with any case, no matter the tone of the case, save only in emergency use of "assists") no further Act is attempted. If a further Act is attempted without first using the first four, the recovery of the case of his own control center will be prolonged or entirely inhibited.

It should be borne in mind that these considerations are of the highest mechanical practicality and are in no way tinged with any mystic quality. They rest on precision reasons of the same order as having to put water near a source of heat to get it to boil.

The Fifth Act is the auditor's ASSESSMENT of the preclear. With a dispassion paralleled in the examination of a horse one might wish to buy, the auditor categorizes the preclear in three echelons of classification as follows:

A. What is the quality of the preclear's reasoning about himself and his environment? About people? This establishes, and seeks only to establish, the degree the preclear's thoughts are controlled by the environment, including other people. Literalness of response to phrases, commands, sudden sounds establishes the preclear on the Tone Scale. What the preclear does about motion, the preclear's muscular tension, the preclear's reaction time all serve to establish the preclear's *thought*.

B. What is the quality of the preclear's *emotion?* This is established by the response of the preclear to the auditor's mood, the voice quality of the preclear, the stability of the preclear's moods. What is the preclear's endocrine state?

C. What is the state of the preclear's *body?* Here the auditor is looking for glaring defects in structure. What is the quality of the preclear's sight, hearing? What is the tonus of the skin and muscles? How are the limbs formed? Is there any chronic "psychosomatic illness"?

This assessment puts the preclear on the Tone Scale. It tells the auditor whether he can use Straightwire, Repetitive Straightwire, Lock Scanning or full Effort. It tells him, as well, what counter-efforts he is most likely to find.

The Sixth Act consists of the establishment of the SERVICE FACSIMILE CHAIN. That service facsimile the auditor must necessarily release can be located by estimating how old the preclear appears to be. The last of the chain is at that age.

It should be heartening to the auditor that his *ability* to perform Acts Five and Six is a lesser factor in his processing. Knowing *how* simply speeds the resolution of the case, for these techniques reach it automatically, without assessment, beyond this point: *The auditor must not Lock Scan or use Effort on preclears below 2.0.* To this end, an auditor must be able to place his preclear on the Tone Scale.

WHEN IN DOUBT, ALWAYS ASSUME THE PRECLEAR IS BELOW 2.0 AND USE ONLY STRAIGHTWIRE AND REPETITIVE STRAIGHTWIRE.

The Seventh Act consists of establishing whether or not the preclear is currently running on his GENETIC CONTROL CENTER. In short, is this a left-hander who has been made right-handed? Fifty percent of all human beings, roughly, are running on the wrong control center.

The Eighth Act consists of STOP, START, CHANGE Straightwire including, in particular, MOVE.

The Ninth Act consists of running EMOTIONAL CURVES until the preclear has the curve of one attempt-failure-engram cycle. This is done until the service facsimile is located.

The Tenth Act consists of running out, by EFFORT, EMOTION and THOUGHT, the service facsimile.

The Eleventh Act consists of running out all SYMPATHY on everyone and anyone in this lifetime, every dynamic. This is done by running the sympathy for its duration, as a lock, over and over until the sympathy is erased. This includes sympathy for self, for every part of the body, for children, for sexual partners, for each parent, for every member of the family, for every ally, for every friend, for every group, organization, state or country, for Man in general, for matter, for energy, for space, for time, for trees and any vegetable life, for bacteria, for cells including sperm, for dogs, cats, horses, cattle, pigs, sheep, game birds, game animals, for souls, spirits, idols, clairvoyants, saints, for the Supreme Being.

The Twelfth Act consists of running, successively, any and all EMOTION on all the dynamics, one after the other. This includes Happiness, Fear, Anger, Boredom, Grief (with or without a tear discharge) and Apathy.

The Thirteenth Act consists of attempting, with THOUGHT, to clear the case of all postulates, evaluations, goals and judgments in the current lifetime.

The Fourteenth Act consists of rehabilitating the proper CONTROL CENTER.

The Fifteenth Act consists of RECHECKING from the Fifth up through the Fourteenth Act, in sequence.

It is apparent that the auditor so far has done minimal Effort Processing. It should also be apparent that most auditors are too ambitious to attack efforts. Experience should tell the auditor that the thorough eradication of the use of a service facsimile chain is not accomplished simply by nullifying one of the facsimiles on that chain. However, as an estimate, by the time the auditor has reached the Tenth Act, the chronic somatic of the case should be out of evidence and should stay out except for new problems and consequences in the environment.

It should also be apparent that with Act Fifteen we have not tapped the reservoirs of the genetic chain. We have not established full memory. We may not have established full perception. The auditor, by the time he has accomplished Act Fifteen, should find himself confronted with a better product than Man has been before. It is definitely in the devotion of the auditor, and within the limits of his time, whether or not he carries his preclear beyond Act Fifteen.

It should be noted that beyond Act Fifteen, potentialities and techniques are either unknown or not established at this time. Up to Act Fifteen, we are on very safe, proven, thoroughly workable ground.

A preclear thoroughly carried through these processes should be classified as a "Fifteen." A preclear carried through to a "chronic somatic release" should be known as a "Ten" (solely for qualification).

THE ESSENCE OF ADVANCED PROCEDURE IS TO FOLLOW IT STEP BY STEP. DO NOT SKIP ANY ACT. DO NOT GO ON TO A FURTHER ACT UNTIL YOU ARE SATISFIED YOU HAVE ACCOMPLISHED THE ACT IN ACTION. DO EVERY ACT THOROUGHLY AND ONLY THEN ADVANCE TO NEXT ACT. THIS SHOULD BE SO THOROUGHLY ESTABLISHED THAT A PRECLEAR, KNOWING ADVANCED PROCEDURE, FINDING AN ACT HAS BEEN INCOMPLETED OR AN ACT SKIPPED, SHOULD JUDGE HIS AUDITOR A SUB-CENTER AT BEST AND GET ANOTHER AUDITOR.

(NOTE: The control center–sub-control center relationship makes husband-wife teams highly inadvisable. Husbands and wives should appear to each other as inviolate personalities, not as auditor and preclear. Three-way teams are far more successful than two-way interchanging teams.)

PRECAUTIONS

"Always be orderly and routine in your commands."

PRECAUTIONS

1. Do not audit a preclear with a technique above his Tone Scale level.

2. Do not audit a preclear with broad techniques until you have resolved the inaccessibility that preclear may have. (This is covered in the sections on accessibility—*Types of Cases* and *Wide-Open and Occluded.*)

3. Do not audit a preclear when he is very tired.

4. Do not audit a preclear who is hungry.

5. Audit preclears who are apparently deficient nutritionally only when you give them nutritional supplements. (This applies to Straightwire and any other process.)

6. Do not audit preclears late at night.

7. Do not evaluate your preclear's data for him.

8. Never back off from a process you have begun.

9. Never give a preclear a second order while he is still attempting the first you gave him.

10. Always be orderly and routine in your commands.

11. Never let your preclear control you. Always be at a level of force short of his objection point.

12. Act like a control center. Never be confused, doubtful or bewildered.

**USE A MINIMUM OF EFFORT PROCESSING
AND THEN ONLY ON SERVICE FACSIMILES.**

THOUGHT

"All thought is preceded by physical effort except Prime Thought, the decision moving the original potential being from the State of Not-Beingness to the State of Beingness."

*T*HOUGHT

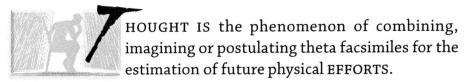

THOUGHT IS the phenomenon of combining, imagining or postulating theta facsimiles for the estimation of future physical EFFORTS.

All thought is preceded by physical effort except PRIME THOUGHT, the decision moving the original potential being from the State of Not-Beingness to the State of Beingness.

Thought is modified by natural purpose.

Natural purpose may or may not be modified, in one lifetime, by past action and efforts. (In other words, thought obeys Prime Static in any one lifetime and can obey it at any moment in that lifetime. Thought is not necessarily stimulus-response.)

Prime Thought occurs at the beginning of the genetic line.

Prime Thought can occur at any moment during any lifetime, moving the individual from the State of Not-Beingness to the State of Beingness. A common name for this phenomenon is "necessity level," although this term is incomplete.

Two broad general processes are indicated:

PROCESS ONE: Causing the preclear to rise, in present time, from the State of Relative Not-Beingness to the State of Vital Beingness.

PROCESS TWO: Clarifying sufficient emotion and effort as well as thought, in the past, to permit the individual to achieve or shift from the State of Relative Not-Beingness to the State of Vital Beingness.

In processing thought, several mechanical processes are used:

STRAIGHTWIRE: (See other publications.)[*]

REPETITIVE STRAIGHTWIRE: Straightwire to one incident, done over and over until the incident is desensitized.

LOCK SCANNING: (See other publications.)[**]

GOAL PROCESSING: (Covered in this manual—*Future Goals.*)

---

[*]See the books *Science of Survival* and *Self Analysis.*
[**]See the books *Science of Survival* and *Handbook for Preclears.*

EMOTION

*"Emotion is a direct index of
the State of Beingness."*

*E*MOTION

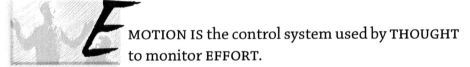

*E*MOTION IS the control system used by THOUGHT to monitor EFFORT.

The endocrine system stands between "I" and the existing or potential effort of the physical being.

The products of the endocrine system catalyze or inhibit the combustion of the carbon-oxygen motor system which is the physical organism.

Emotion is a direct index of the State of Beingness.

When badly aberrated, the physical being gives the appearance of monitoring, through emotion, "I".

When in acceptable condition, the organism is monitored through the endocrine system by its control center.

Emotion was evolved by motion. Motion of the physical organism is monitored by emotion.

Emotion can be processed directly in its own echelon. During such processing, the preclear strays into thought and effort.

SYMPATHY is commonly accepted to mean the posing of an emotional state similar to the emotional state of an individual in Grief or Apathy. This is a secondary reaction and has its own peculiarity, but is nevertheless on the Tone Scale between 0.9 and 0.4. Sympathy follows or is based upon *overt action* by the preclear.

SYMPATHY can be mechanically considered as the posing of any emotion so as to be similar to the emotion of another. This, in view of popular usage, should have a special designation: "comparitism."

THE EMOTIONAL CURVE is the drop from any position above 2.0 to a position below 2.0 on the realization of failure or inadequacy. It is easily recovered by preclears. It leads straight into service facsimiles. It should be handled as an emotion lock and run over and over, until desensitized, wherever it can be found.

THE REVERSE CURVE is the emotional curve rising from below 2.0 to above 2.0. It happens in a short space of time. It is important because it locates allies.

Appreciation of existence depends upon the free use, by "I", of emotion. Emotional states, no matter how rapidly, should be postulated by "I".

FREEING THE EMOTION ON ANY CASE IS A VITAL AND NECESSARY OPERATION.

The preclear does not have to be tripped into severe secondaries, into engrams or even computations to free his emotion.

EFFORT

"The static of Life handles motion."

EFFORT

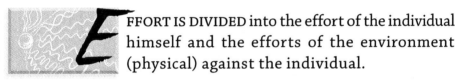FFORT IS DIVIDED into the effort of the individual himself and the efforts of the environment (physical) against the individual.

The individual's own effort is simply called EFFORT.

The efforts of the environment are called COUNTER-EFFORTS.

There is a physical effort behind every computation except Prime Thought.

The static of Life handles motion. It is capable of starting, stopping and changing motion. These starts, stops and changes are, each one, physical efforts.

All the counter-efforts the body has ever received are evidently in store. Every physical effort of the organism has been at some time a counter-effort.

Counter-efforts are not necessarily inhibitive to survival.

To hold any counter-effort requires the self-determinism of the organism.

IT IS NOT THE PURPOSE OF PROCESSING TO EXHAUST ALL COUNTER-EFFORTS FROM THE ORGANISM.

THE PURPOSE OF PROCESSING IS TO REHABILITATE THE SELF-DETERMINISM OF THE ORGANISM ABOUT COUNTER-EFFORTS.

So long as an organism can employ a counter-effort in its survival, that counter-effort is not aberrative.

Counter-efforts become aberrative only when they have been chosen by the organism for non-survival usages or when the organism was unable to employ them for survival, as in the genetic blueprint and experience.

EXCESS COUNTER-EFFORTS are those which have not been employed and could not be handled by the organism. These are not classed with DEATH EFFORTS, as death efforts (counter-efforts) are primary genetic data all along the track.

Excess counter-efforts present themselves easily. They can be processed out. But they are of no primary concern to the auditor.

THE ONLY REASON AN AUDITOR PROCESSES EFFORT IS TO REGAIN ABERRATIVE POSTULATES.

THE ONLY EFFORTS THE AUDITOR PROCESSES ARE IN THE SERVICE FACSIMILE CHAIN.

The only thing of value to recover from an engram is the effort. And the only reason one recovers the effort is to recover the postulates the individual himself made during the engram. And the only engrams one processes are on the service facsimile chain and it is not necessary to process any more of these than to let the preclear let go of the chain.

If one sees an obvious deficiency in the preclear (glasses, deafness, baldness, thinness, etc.), he can request the effort the preclear must make to be deficient (have poor eyesight, hearing, baldness, etc.).

THE ONLY ABERRATIVE EFFORTS ARE NON-SURVIVAL EFFORTS.

Efforts exist within the efforts within the efforts within the efforts, much on the order of a picture of a picture within a picture within a picture, etc.

By calling for "efforts to have efforts," the preclear can be taken all the way back on the time track to Prime Thought.

A preclear can be trained into feeling efforts by coaxing him to make one in present time and then re-experience it.

The auditor must know about efforts and counter-efforts. He can do much with them and much of what he can do is startling and bizarre. Efforts contain perceptics. If you run an effort long enough, you can recover perceptics from it in most cases.

You will find it difficult to run an effort against the postulate to "keep the effort."

There are countless billions of efforts and counter-efforts in any case.

The main thing the auditor can do wrong about effort is to run too much effort or to think effort is more important than thought, which it is not.

You cannot rehabilitate an organism chemically to any degree. You cannot rehabilitate it with effort. Wrong side of the board.

THE ONLY EFFORTS ARE TO START, STOP AND CHANGE, NOT TO START, NOT TO STOP, NOT TO CHANGE.

Happiness is applied individual effort. Apathy is no effort, all counter-effort. Other efforts and counter-efforts range the Tone Scale in the degree that the individual is handling the current effort in the service facsimile.

EFFORT PROCESSING

"Effort Processing is done by running moments of physical stress. These are run either as simple efforts or counter-efforts ..."

EFFORT PROCESSING

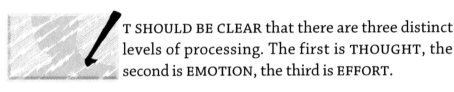

*I*T SHOULD BE CLEAR that there are three distinct levels of processing. The first is THOUGHT, the second is EMOTION, the third is EFFORT.

Each has its own particular skill.

THOUGHT is done by Straightwire, Repetitive Straightwire and Lock Scanning, and is directed toward concepts of conclusions or evaluations or actual precise moments where the preclear evaluated or concluded.

EMOTION is done by Straightwire, Lock Scanning and Lock and Engram and Secondary Running, with the total address to emotion. A moment of sympathy, of determinism, of defiance, of agreement is run just as though the incident were an engram—which is to say, the preclear is made to re-experience the emotion and, incidentally, a few perceptics, over and over from beginning to end until the emotion is off the lock.

EFFORT PROCESSING is done by running moments of physical stress. These are run either as simple efforts or counter-efforts or as whole precise incidents. Such incidents as those which contain physical pain or heavy stress of motion (such as injuries, accidents or illnesses) are addressed by Effort Processing.

It should be seen, then, that we have three levels of operation.

The most intimate is THOUGHT. An individual evaluates or concludes a certain thing. He is thereafter bound by his conclusion. He has caused an effect of which he is the recipient. If such a thought is recalled over and over until it is thoroughly desensitized, emotions and efforts resulting from such a postulate fall away. The individual lets go of the facsimile and it is no longer effective upon him, if the postulate tended to use a facsimile to make it effective.

THOUGHT communicates its decisions to body and environment by use of the EMOTION. Thought is intimately in contact with the trigger mechanisms of emotion and might be said to rule through emotion. Via emotion, thought causes physical action and reaction to take place. To accomplish such physical action and reaction, thought uses earlier experiences (facsimiles) and utilizes their motion, effort and counter-effort to cause activity on the part of the body and environment.

Thus EMOTION is a bridge which is used by THOUGHT to effect EFFORT. Take away or desensitize the emotion and one has again disconnected facsimiles (of any kind) from the organism and the organism and its thought are not effected any longer by the facsimile.

Thought can seem to be smothered in emotion in that it is necessary in most cases to unburden emotion from the case in order to discover many major and vital evaluations and conclusions. By unburdening the case of emotion, evaluations and conclusions long lost to view, but still effective, come to light and are desensitized. Thought, self-determined originally, may postulate conflictingly from time to time with resultant failures, sympathies and other mis-emotions.

Mis-emotion then "smothers" the motor control panels and hides the postulates. Thus the running of emotion is done to lay bare past postulates and evaluations which are the actual sources of aberration and the suspended pain, which has been called in the past "psychosomatic illness" and is called here, in this science, CHRONIC SOMATICS (somatic meaning "physical state").

A heavy, painful facsimile need not itself be exhausted, for it is held in place primarily by the preclear's desire (past postulate, not agreeing with present environment) and this postulate is smothered by emotion. Run the emotion, discover and desensitize the postulate and the facsimile ordinarily drops away and does not further concern the preclear. Further, he does not substitute another ache or pain for it because the original reason for the facsimile (past postulate) is gone.

Effort Processing is applied to heavy facsimiles. It happens occasionally that the effort on a facsimile is so heavy that it occludes the emotion, which in turn occludes the thought. Thus, enough effort must be recovered to lay bare the emotion so as to get at the postulates and desensitize them. A heavy facsimile is thus treated by Effort Processing in order to free the emotion and thus the postulates.

THE FACSIMILE IS NOT TREATED TO COMPLETE EXHAUSTION BUT ONLY TO THE POINT WHERE THE EMOTION AND THOUGHT ARE REACHED. IT THEN SHOULD FALL INTO DISUSE AND IT DOES NOT MATTER THAT EFFORT IS LEFT ON IT.

The last thing which is done to the heavy facsimile is, of course, to pick up the preclear's agreement with the auditor to run it and the emotion of "determinism" involved in the running itself. Otherwise, the facsimile may remain somewhat in force. This is done by Lock Running or Lock Scanning.

A heavy facsimile used to be known as an "engram." In view of the fact that it has been found to be stored elsewhere than in the cells, the term "heavy facsimile" has now come into use.

A HEAVY FACSIMILE is an experience, complete with all perceptions and emotions and thoughts and efforts, occupying a precise place in space and a moment in time. It can be an operation, an injury, a term of heavy physical exertion or even a death. It is composed of the preclear's own effort and the effort of the environment (counter-effort). The emotion of a heavy facsimile is marked by the thoroughness with which the counter-efforts have overcome the preclear.

Thus, total overcoming of the preclear's own effort by the counter-effort is Apathy. Less thoroughly overcome, the preclear's own effort is in Grief. Even less thoroughly overcome, the preclear is in Fear. Even less counter-effort and more preclear effort results in Anger. When the preclear's own effort is greater than the counter-efforts, the emotion is Antagonism. As the counter-effort is slighter and more diffuse, but the preclear's effort is not punitive, Boredom results as the emotion. When the preclear's own effort is punitive and successful against counter-efforts, we have varying degrees of happiness and effectiveness.

Thus the tone of any individual or any heavy facsimile is established by the response to the environmental effort. And this response varies from no effort, all counter-effort to all effort, slight counter-effort. This is made up into a Tone Scale which goes from 0.0 for the lowest condition, to 20.0 at optimum condition and then dwindling activity to 40.0 for a top static, the bottom static being Death.

Effort
Processing

An individual may be so involved in combating a heavy facsimile, which is chronically with him, that he is chronically ill. Holding on to a chronic facsimile, the preclear has certain pattern responses and aberrations. In a facsimile where he is overwhelmed by motion, he is listless and Apathetic. In one where the forces balance, he is in Anger, etc.

The auditor, in an occluded case, may find it necessary to open the case by running Effort Processing. He looks at his preclear to discover some obvious physical aberration. This is held in place by a counter-effort. The auditor simply asks, "If your (head) were being pushed, which way would it be moving?" (Or a leg, or some otherwise deformed area.) The counter-effort is right there, waiting. The preclear answers with a direction. The auditor then asks the preclear to feel his (head) moving against the counter-effort. A somatic will turn on. The auditor simply continues to ask for the various efforts and counter-efforts. Perceptions quite ordinarily fall out of the effort. A whole incident may come to view. This is the *heavy facsimile* and also the *chronic facsimile*. It is also a *service facsimile*. There is no sending the preclear around on his time track. He is right there in the heavy facsimile.

The facsimile thus uncovered is run until its emotion can be recovered. This is then scanned off until the postulates appear and these are then desensitized. The preclear's own thoughts and postulates are the aberration source. What is said to him is simply evaluation causing him, at times, to postulate.

THE AUDITOR HAS NO CONCERN FOR WHAT IS SAID, FOR REPEATER TECHNIQUE, FOR PERCEPTIONS—SAVE ONLY IN THAT THEY MAY SLIGHTLY AID THE RECOVERY OF THE EMOTION.

There are many tricks in Effort Processing. An auditor can ask for the "effort to do" or "be" anything and the preclear can work it out. There is an automatic response mechanism which gives forth the proper effort for the question—an interesting and reliable phenomenon. An auditor could take a dictionary and simply begin asking for any and all efforts suggested to him by the dictionary. However, using Effort Processing to this extent is neither indicated nor even broadly useful.

EVERY EFFORT IS IN A NON-SURVIVAL DIRECTION IN THAT IT WAS ONCE A COUNTER-EFFORT.

One can get the effort within the effort within the effort and have his preclear back into the genetic line at a swift rate. For efforts and counter-efforts are the stuff of which the blueprint of the human body itself is made. There are two cellular lines going back from the shellfish stage, for at this stage two cell lines become a team. The ancestors of this stage (before this point) go back into two separate experience stages. One can take a preclear, all unsuspecting of anything but the "lived only once theory," and throw him back with "efforts within efforts" into some remarkable experiences. This is a biologist's dream, for he can look at original forms and trace genetic lines in individuals who may not even know of evolution. The genetic facsimiles of the whole evolution chain are on file and have thus been discovered. This should not be too surprising. For the blueprint had to be somewhere and, in efforts, it has been discovered and a trail blazed along its track. The problems of the initial photon converters, the "missing link" between the vertebrate and invertebrate stages can be located, amongst other items of interest. The simple locating of "efforts to make efforts" throws anyone back down the long line. In ordinary processing, this is not ordinarily used.

EFFORT
PROCESSING

The number of efforts and counter-efforts is vast, beyond count, and contain the whole physical experience. The body is composed of efforts and counter-efforts. In theory, if they were all run out, the preclear would vanish. Fortunately, this is not necessary for processing.

THE BASIC EFFORTS ARE NOT TO BE, TO BE.

THESE RESOLVE INTO THE EFFORTS TO START, TO STOP, TO CHANGE, NOT TO START, NOT TO STOP AND NOT TO CHANGE.

THE BASIC GOALS ARE TO REMAIN IN A STATE OF REST AGAINST COUNTER-EFFORT AND TO REMAIN IN A STATE OF MOTION AGAINST COUNTER-EFFORTS.

Newton's laws would apply—and we would have "stimulus-response" thinking—except for the ability of the mind to interpose self-determined action and motion despite stimuli or disregarding it.

There are efforts to have affinity, efforts to have communication, efforts to have agreement and reality. There are efforts to see and not to see, to hear and not to hear. There are efforts to do or not to do anything.

By VALENCE is meant "identity." When the preclear switches from his own valence to another valence, he is actually taking the position of a counter-effort against himself. In his own valence, he exerts his own efforts. In a counter-effort valence, he exerts counter-effort against himself. In a dental operation under general anesthetic, the preclear's own effort becomes so nulled that he takes the counter-effort. Then he recalls the incident out of valence (as the dentist or the nurse or, quite irrationally, even the dental tools or the bed) and hurts himself.

(Self-auditing is done, ordinarily, out of valence and results in the preclear expending counter-efforts against himself. Thus he succeeds only in hurting himself.)

The NO-EFFORT STATE is the state in which counter-effort is overwhelming the individual. Thus the auditor finds the case in Apathy at a no-effort point. Every heavy facsimile has points for any point on the Tone Scale and thus the preclear can hang up in a place where he can have no effort of his own. The auditor solves this by running out the counter-effort until it is sufficiently null to rehabilitate the preclear's own effort. (Some testing still remains on this particular point of Effort Processing.)

A service facsimile is very resistive to Effort Processing, ordinarily. The auditor must remember to run the emotion as soon as possible and get the matter into good recall so that the postulates can be run. That should be the end of the service facsimile or at least one of its chain. Effort Processing is not an end in itself, but an end toward recovering emotion so that one can recover thought. Effort Processing should be thoroughly understood by an auditor and should then be minimally used.

A preclear who cannot re-experience an effort can be educated into the ability by causing him to make a present time effort and then recalling it. He will shortly discover that efforts can be re-experienced. Various efforts can then be run.

It is sometimes much easier to get a case to run emotion than to run effort. This should be done, by all means, for emotion is closer to thought than is effort.

DON'T USE EFFORTS ON LOW-TONED PRECLEARS.

POSTULATES

"Postulates are made and are effective on every dynamic."

POSTULATES

 POSTULATE IS that self-determined THOUGHT which starts, stops or changes past, present or future EFFORTS.

Postulates alone aberrate the individual.

By setting forth any postulate, the individual a moment later is being effected by his own cause. The postulate becomes unworkable in a radically changed environment, but may remain effective.

Old people are generally considered to be "set in their ways." It would be more accurate to say that they were "set in their own postulates."

The only reason an individual uses service facsimiles lies in his self-determined postulate to use them.

It is necessary to make postulates. To make postulates and handle them, it is necessary to handle past postulates.

A postulate may spring from past effort or Prime Thought.

A PRIME POSTULATE is the decision to change from a State of Not-Beingness to a State of Beingness.

A Prime Postulate can occur at any time without regard to past or present effort, since theta is always present in a non-facsimiled condition.

Except for a very strong Prime Postulate, early postulates are effective over later postulates.

A Prime Postulate has the effect of cancelling not only past postulates, but the past individual as well (when it is strong).

A NEGATIVE POSTULATE is the postulate "not to be." It cancels past postulates and it also cancels, in greater or lesser degree, the entire individual. The track earlier than a negative postulate is largely occluded. It is as virgin as a Prime Postulate.

An individual who has made a postulate on a subject experiences "failure" when he has to make an OPPOSITE POSTULATE later. The opposite postulate has the effect of a negative postulate. The opposite postulate is distinguished from a negative postulate because it depends upon effort, which a negative postulate does not necessarily have to do.

Any preclear can be quickly shown, when he has reached the Fourth Act, that he himself determined his own condition. This is not done accusatively.

The auditor can show the preclear in many ways that the preclear is capable of postulating himself into changed condition. The preclear ordinarily, at the very least, can recall when he postulated himself ill to get out of going to school or out of an engagement.

Postulates, whenever made, are responsible for the condition of the preclear—bad or good.

Because postulates are made in moments of physical stress, at times, and are very forceful when so made, engrams (heavy facsimiles) occasionally must be entered. But because Prime Postulates occur, it is not necessary to go too early to get effective postulates for this lifetime desensitized from a case.

Postulates made by a preclear are a pattern. It is necessary to reach the earliest postulates by touching the later ones and running them back with Straightwire.

Postulates surrender just like any other lock or, in engrams, just like any other perception in an engram.

AUDITING A PRECLEAR FORCEFULLY AGAINST POSTULATES HE HAS MADE TO THE CONTRARY, MAKES HIM SUBJECT TO OPPOSITE POSTULATES AND DRIVES HIM INTO APATHY.

Thus such postulates are a matter of first address. These include postulates "not to be treated by doctors" and postulates "not to change."

"Agreement to be processed" is a postulate which must be picked up eventually.

POSTULATES ARE MADE AND ARE EFFECTIVE ON EVERY DYNAMIC.

POSTULATES ARE REDUCED SYSTEMATICALLY FOR EVERY DYNAMIC.

THE POSTULATES THE AUDITOR WANTS ARE THOSE APPERTAINING TO THE RETENTION AND USE BY THE PRECLEAR OF HIS SERVICE FACSIMILE CHAIN.

EVALUATION

*"Postulates are made because
of Evaluations."*

EVALUATION

POSTULATES ARE made because of EVALUATIONS. Postulates ordinarily do not lift unless the *reason why* is also contacted. This is brief but very important.

TYPES OF CASES
Past, Present and Future

*"A High-Tone individual thinks
wholly into the future."*

$\mathcal{T}$YPES OF CASES
Past, Present and Future

 VERY CALCULATION of effort made by the mind is directed toward future.

The individual compares conditions in the PAST to observations in the PRESENT in order to calculate efforts in the FUTURE.

A HIGH-TONE individual thinks wholly into the future. He is extroverted toward his environment. He clearly observes the environment with full perception, unclouded by undistinguished fears about the environment. He thinks very little about himself, but operates automatically in his own interests. He enjoys existence. His calculations (postulations and evaluations) are swift and accurate. He is very self-confident. He *knows* he knows and does not even bother to assert that he knows. He controls his environment.

The so-called NORMAL is used here to be at around 2.5 or 3.0 on the Tone Scale. He is partially extroverted, partially introverted. He spends considerable time with his calculations. He evaluates slowly even when he has the data and then postulates without realizing too much about his postulation.

He has much in the past which he does not care to recall. He has much in his present which gives him concern. His future goals are rather well nullified by future fears. He is Homo sapiens. He is in terrible condition taken from the viewpoint of Homo novis. He is in excellent condition from the viewpoint of past -ologies. He controls some of his environment, but is mainly controlled by that environment. He is somewhat of a liability in interpersonal relations, demanding ARC and feeling he cannot live without it. He understands that he understands some things.

The NEUROTIC is considered to be below 2.5. The neurotic has thorough concern about the future to the degree that he has many more fears about the future than he has goals in the future. He spends much of his time pondering the past. He acts and then wonders if he has acted correctly and is sure he has not. Thoughts to him are as solid as MEST. He is overwhelmed by sudden counter-efforts. He is operating on a sub-control center which has been itself very blunted. He is ill much of the time, to a greater or lesser degree. He has colds. He brings "bad luck" and disaster. He is Homo sapiens at his "rational worst."

The DRAMATIZING PSYCHOTIC is not always looked upon as insane. Whether or not he is classified as insane depends upon whether or not he is of obvious menace to other Homo sapiens. He is fixed in one facsimile which he plays over and over to the environment around him. He is controlled by his environment to the extent that anything in his environment turns on his dramatization. He is disastrous to have around. Inaccessible persons passing for "normals" are sometimes dramatizing psychotics who dramatize infrequently—perhaps only once or twice a day. The dramatizing psychotic lives mainly in the illusion of his own facsimile with its surroundings, not actual surroundings. He is definitely not in present time at any time.

The COMPUTING PSYCHOTIC passes quite commonly for a "normal." Here, the individual is taking dictation solely from a facsimile of some past moment of pain and is acting upon the advice of that "circuit" and is calling it thought. The psychotic personality is distinguished by its irrationality and its perversion of values. An inaccessible "normal" is usually a computing psychotic. Thoughts are MEST to the computing psychotic. To take away or relieve a computation is like removing physical matter from the person. The computing psychotic lives wholly in the past and has no future. He cannot be interested in future goals. Often he does not even have future fears. His concerns are with past decisions, but he cannot even make a decision for the past. Most computing psychotics are not in institutions or under any restraint. Only those computing psychotics who are obviously and dramatically dangerous to their fellow Homo sapiens are labeled psychotic by past -ologies. Many esteemed and respected Homo sapiens in many professions are yet computing psychotics who operate, puppet-like, on installed knowledge. The distinguishing characteristic of the computing psychotic is his utter inability to change his mind. He may even make a cult or a virtue out of "consistency."

THE MOST COMMON MISTAKE AN AUDITOR CAN MAKE IN HIS EVALUATION OF A PRECLEAR IS TO MISDETERMINE A COMPUTING PSYCHOTIC AS A NORMAL.

The clue that he has made a mistake is his discovery of the difficulty he has in getting the computing psychotic to get up any locks. Another clue is inaccessibility. Intelligence is *no* clue to the computing psychotic. Neither is dress, nor manners and learning, since these can also be used by the circuit. Inaccessibility, heaviness of locks—these are the clues.

The degree of extroversion of the preclear and, with that, his ability to face future threats and reach toward future goals determine his height on the Tone Scale.

Above 2.5, the preclear thinks about the future. From there down to 1.0, he thinks mainly about the present and has some dread of both future and past. Below 1.0, he is wholly concerned with the past. During any one session, the auditor has a preclear all over the Tone Scale. He should leave him extroverted. Any lock chain, for instance, should be scanned only to extroversion on that chain—scanning further drops the preclear into another chain, thus re-introverting him. The temporary extroversion and introversion is momentary and incidental.

THE AUDITOR IS PRINCIPALLY CONCERNED WITH CHRONIC ASPECT AS OUTLINED ABOVE.

WIDE-OPEN AND OCCLUDED

"The Occluded case complains of illness ordinarily. The Wide-Open case commonly insists upon how well he is. Both are errors."

*W*IDE-OPEN
AND OCCLUDED

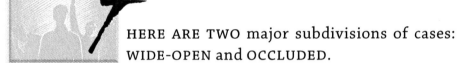

HERE ARE TWO major subdivisions of cases: WIDE-OPEN and OCCLUDED.

At this time it is imperfectly understood why there is such a difference. There are many clues and much data, but a static conclusion is not advisable at this time.

The WIDE-OPEN case is possessed of full perception except somatic, which is probably light even to the point of anesthesia. Wide-open does not refer to a high-tone individual, but to one below 2.5 who *should* be easy to work but is often inaccessible and who finds it difficult to regain a somatic and simple to regain perception.

It is pointed out that perceptions are rather easily drained from facsimiles, leaving the effort still in place. It is also pointed out that the wide-open case is often incapable of much effort in present time. Thus the perceptions of the wide-open case may be simply curtained, in some fashion, from his effort. The wide-open case can be a computing psychotic. This matter is dangerous to the auditor, for he may think a wide-open case is a high-tone case with full perception.

THE WIDE-OPEN CASE CAN BE STUCK IN AN ARDUOUS FACSIMILE AND, BY RUNNING HEAVY INCIDENTS, MAY BE DRIVEN WHOLLY PSYCHOTIC.

This is almost the only danger in this science.

The WIDE-OPEN case is handled by an address to thought and emotion, not to effort. It should be scouted carefully to find out if the case will Lock Scan. This is determined by how easy it is to run one lock, how easily that lock blows. An auditor can Lock Scan a wide-open case into a heavy effort facsimile and stick him there.

The wide-open case is very literal, as is any low-toned case, to words. Words and any other symbols are almost MEST. The wide-open case often makes a fetish from symbols. This is an escape mechanism. "Dream therapy" and so forth are the dreams of low-toned cases.

The OCCLUDED case is fixed, most likely, in the effort of a heavy facsimile. Thought and emotion, rather than effort, are best applied to this case until a computation is reached.

The occluded case is using a service facsimile so heavily that it is in constant restimulation and that service facsimile is occluded by heavy effort. In contrast, the service facsimile of the wide-open case may be concentrated on perception with its effort avoided.

The OCCLUDED case complains of illness ordinarily.

The WIDE-OPEN case commonly insists upon how well he is.

Both are errors.

COMPUTATIONS

"Every Homo sapiens is running on aberrated Computations."

COMPUTATIONS

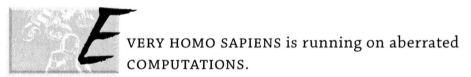EVERY HOMO SAPIENS is running on aberrated COMPUTATIONS.

The COMPUTATION, technically, is that aberrated evaluation and postulate that one must be consistently in a certain state in order to succeed. The computation thus may mean that one must "entertain in order to be alive" or that one must "be dignified in order to succeed" or that one must "own much in order to live."

A COMPUTATION IS SIMPLY STATED. IT IS ALWAYS ABERRATED. IT IS COMMONLY IN CONFLICT WITH BASIC GOAL.

BASIC GOAL is that goal native to the personality for a lifetime. It is second only in importance to survival itself. It is incident to the individuation of the person. A child of two knows its basic goal. It is compounded from genetic generations of experience. It can be found and reduced in some long past heavy effort facsimile, such as death. It is neither advisable nor inadvisable to tamper with it. Much experience aligns on it. Desensitized, it would be supplanted by another basic goal.

A computation is generally a this-lifetime affair and it is intimately concerned with the service facsimiles of this lifetime.

Some computations are so thoroughly irrational that they vanish at a glance. These include "I have to be late to be early," "I have to be angry to people to be liked." They are contradictory.

A computation is as insidious as it pretends to align with survival or, in other words, as it seems to match the environment.

NO COMPUTATION IS COMPATIBLE WITH SKILL AND DATA. A "COMPUTATION" COMPATIBLE WITH SKILL AND DATA *IS* BASIC GOAL.

A man whose every ability lies in a dignified and smooth area may yet have a computation that he must "be a clown." One with the basic goal of entertaining may yet feel he must "be dignified." Contradictoriness is *essence* in computations.

ALL COMPUTATIONS ARE NON-SURVIVAL.

The computation lies in earlier postulates of this lifetime, or lifetimes, post–basic goal. (It is treated for this lifetime only, in order to achieve a Fifteen.)

Computations are established by noting activities or ideas of the preclear out of agreement with his skills and abilities.

Computations clarify by address to service facsimiles.

COMPUTATIONS ARE HELD IN PLACE WHOLLY TO INVALIDATE OTHERS.

SERVICE
FACSIMILES

"A Service Facsimile is that facsimile which the preclear uses to apologize for his failures."

SERVICE FACSIMILES

THE MAIN GOAL of the auditor is to locate and release SERVICE FACSIMILES for this lifetime.

There is ordinarily but one actual service facsimile on a case. But this one is accompanied by before and after heavy facsimiles and locks.

A SERVICE FACSIMILE is that facsimile which the preclear uses to apologize for his failures. In other words, it is used to make others wrong and procure their cooperation in the survival of the preclear.

If the preclear *well* cannot achieve survival, he attempts an illness or disability as a survival computation.

The workability and necessity of the service facsimile is only superficially useful.

The service facsimile is an action method of withdrawing from a State of Beingness to a State of Not-Beingness and is intended to persuade others to coax the individual back into a State of Beingness.

The service facsimile has a complete and explicit anatomy. It begins with an effort to control along any dynamic, with a failure to control, with a recognition of the failure, with a postulate to be ill, injured or unable, continues with an illness, injury or inability and may or may not end (short of processing) in days, weeks, years or an entire lifetime.

Hysterical deafness, blindness, colds, any chronic somatic, any aberrated behavior pattern is the content of service facsimiles.

The inception of the earliest service facsimile for this lifetime is usually between six months and three years of age. It has many locks.

It is located by running the EMOTIONAL CURVE.

It is then exhausted with complete processing, which includes thought, emotion and effort. Its companions later on the chain are then similarly reduced.

ALL THAT IS WRONG WITH ANY CASE IS A SERVICE FACSIMILE. DISCOVER AND REDUCE THE SERVICE FACSIMILE AND ITS CHAIN AND THE AUDITOR CHANGES THE NATURE OF MAN AND PROMOTES HIM. AN INDIVIDUAL WHO HAS NO SERVICE FACSIMILE WILL NOT ACCUMULATE FACSIMILES TO HIS HARM OR BECOME RESTIMULATED BY OTHERS.

The heart of auditing is the service facsimile.

DRAMATIZATIONS

"A Dramatization is like a record which can be played over and over."

DRAMATIZATIONS

THE INDIVIDUAL STILL POSSESSED of service facsimiles DRAMATIZES them.

He may dramatize them in or out of valence.

A DRAMATIZATION is like a record which can be played over and over.

Dramatizing is an apology for failure.

SYMPATHY EXCITERS

"Sympathy Exciters are most commonly parents, allies and pets."

$\mathcal{S}$YMPATHY EXCITERS

**A** SYMPATHY EXCITER is any entity on any dynamic for which the individual has felt sympathy of the variety between 0.9 and 0.4.

Sympathy is an excellent occluder and valence shifter. It also involves and freezes the emotion of the individual.

The ordinary course of action leading to sympathy is action against the entity which will be sympathized with, or action against an entity earlier than the sympathy exciter.

Sympathy is a non-survival apology for action against entities on any dynamic, which action has failed.

A sympathy exciter is easily located in any case. There are many in every case.

The auditor can enter the sympathy chain from many angles. One is to locate "Who (the individual) has been mean to?" Another is "When did you fail to control another by action?" Another is simply "For whom have you felt sympathy?"

SYMPATHY EXCITERS are most commonly parents, allies and pets.

Childhood stories are cunningly laid traps for sympathy. Such stories, poems or songs affect a case strongly, but are locks for actual control efforts (which have failed) on the part of the child against any entity on any dynamic. Sympathy should be run from such stories.

SYMPATHY is run as a heavy facsimile. It is run without verbalization. It is run without accompanying effort. It is always run *with the reason* one was sympathetic. It is run over and over until the preclear extroverts. It may be run from late to early or early to late, wherever it can be found.

SYMPATHY MUST BE TAKEN WHOLLY OFF THE CASE.

PRESENT TIME PROBLEMS

"All cases have one or many actual
Present Time Problems."

PRESENT TIME PROBLEMS

ALL CASES HAVE one or many actual PRESENT TIME PROBLEMS.

It is most compatible with low-tone cases to "strip" a present time problem as the first action (Act Four) in actual processing. The neurotic has most of his concentration on the present. He is afraid of it. His concentration is so heavily on the present that he cannot research the past and he certainly cannot bear much of the future, either as to its fears or goals.

The NEUROTIC CASE is therefore entered with the mechanism of stripping a present time problem at the point of Act Four.

STRIPPING PRESENT TIME is a simple operation. Once one has established communication with the preclear, he is invited to discuss his present time. All by itself, this is "therapeutic." Simply permitting a man to tell you of his operations is "therapeutic," even if it compares in value with actual processing to collecting a grain of sand when one can sweep the Sahara.

The "confessional" is simply the address to present time problems. And although the recipient of the confession does nothing more than assure that "all is forgiven," the individual feels better. This, by the way, is the only cross between this science and past efforts at therapy.

The action of stripping is done by taking every aspect of every factor in the problem and running it back to the postulate the preclear made to be concerned about that aspect of the factor.

The auditor must beware of being too monotonous with his "When did you first decide that _____?" He should take pains to vary his patter: "Let's see if we can find some earlier material on this." "Did you ever know anyone who is like your wife?"

BE HUMAN EVEN IF HUMAN NOVIS. THE AUDITOR IS INTERESTED IN THE CURRENT TRAVAIL OF THIS HOMO SAPIENS.

The preclear will not unburden if he thinks the auditor will violate his confidence. He will not unburden if the auditor has no regard for the possible severity of the problem.

The auditor's main concern is adroitly preventing the preclear from wandering off the actual factors of the problem. The preclear is liable to ramble. The auditor should not fear to interrupt this rambling.

The auditor does not give advice or straighten out the preclear's present time. He makes the preclear's present time bearable by desensitizing the past it restimulates.

The cleverness of the auditor is devoted, alertly, to the calculation of the actual problem and leading the preclear into past similar concerns and his postulates to make it a problem.

The address to the present time problem should be discontinued immediately that the preclear is obviously less concerned with it. The present time problem will not wholly vanish. The auditor is simply using the mechanism to get the preclear into a better swing of processing.

Addressing the present time problem (PROBLEM, for short) is a therapy in itself, if we desire therapies. Get at the factors of real concern, get a postulate or two off about them, run a little emotion, use some MEST Processing about the factors and prepare, thus, the case for the Fifth Act. Resolving the present time problem makes a better Homo sapiens. It does not much advance a case in view of how far that case can be advanced. However, a clever and quick auditor could probably make his fortune using only this technique and by it prevent divorces, cure colds, save jobs, accidents and illnesses. It is only a very minor miracle and should be regarded as such.

PROBLEM PROCESSING CAN BE DWELT UPON OVERLONG BY THE AUDITOR AND SHOULD BE USED ONLY LONG ENOUGH TO PREVENT THE PRECLEAR FROM BEING TOO DISTRACTED FROM THE MAIN TASK BY HIS ENVIRONMENT.

PAST PROBLEMS

"Here, the problem is one of coaxing the preclear to make an evaluation on each of the factors involved in the past problem and then, finally, a conclusion on the problem."

PAST PROBLEMS

*T*HE PSYCHOTIC is suspended in a decision, unmade, about a PAST PROBLEM.

The unwillingness to make this decision and the conflict of factors thus results in a confusion in the past severe enough to cause a FAILURE IN DECISION or an ABSENCE OF POSTULATE.

Here, the problem is one of coaxing the preclear to make an evaluation on each of the factors involved in the past problem and then, finally, a conclusion on the problem.

This is very simple to resolve. It may not be simple to locate. Simple ARC is used until the problem presents itself.

THE AUDITOR DOES NOT ADVISE AN EVALUATION OR A CONCLUSION. WHEN HE DOES SO, HE IS LOCKING ON TOP OF EVERY OTHER ADVICE WHICH THE PRECLEAR HAS RECEIVED. THE AUDITOR IS SIMPLY TRYING TO GET THE PRECLEAR TO USE HIS OWN COMPUTER. COMPUTATIONS ARE EFFECTED FIRST BY EVALUATION AND THEN BY CONCLUSION. IF THE AUDITOR DOES MORE THAN LEAD, THE PRECLEAR HAS NOT USED HIS OWN COMPUTER AND HAS NOT RESOLVED THE PROBLEM.

This, in essence, by the way, is why hypnotism does not, repeat does not, never has, repeat never has worked and never will work, since it is the environment (the hypnotist) making a series of decisions for the subject. Your preclear, when he is hung up in a past decision failure, is in a hypnotic state anyway—for he has to be that low on the scale to be so confused.

In handling men, you can put them in a hypnotic, automaton state by posing rapidly a series of factors they then see they cannot of themselves evaluate and then getting them to a point where they are in an anxiety for you to make the decision. Depress them low enough in this wise and they obey like robots.

THUS DON'T RUIN YOUR PRECLEAR.

FUTURE GOALS

*"Future goals take care of themselves when
the preclear moves out into Beingness."*

FUTURE GOALS

 MAN WITHOUT FUTURE GOALS is a worried and sick man.

The reason why an individual cannot approach a future goal or even strongly postulate one, lies in his inability to resolve the present or to make a decision in the past.

The future goal may be cancelled by fears for the future.

A case can be worked by alternately seeking to discover the preclear's future goals and then locating the fears that these goals cannot be attained, and by locating and reducing the postulates and emotions which cause the fears.

A CASE WHICH WILL NOT TELL YOU, AT LEAST IN PART, A FUTURE GOAL OR AMBITION IS PSYCHOTIC.

Even a neurotic will have some fragments of future goals and will discuss them. A case which will not discuss future goals is hung up in a past decision conflict and should be worked in that area (the past) as the case isn't even in present time, no matter how it may seem to conform or converse or "be charming."

The auditor who discovers this condition in a preclear can make the error of seeking to strip postulates which inhibit postulating future goals or create future fears. He can also err when confronted by this condition, by trying to process present time. This preclear has enormous apparent present time problems, certainly. They are all hung up on a past failure to decide.

The GOALLESS CASE has shuddered so far away from decision that he is also departed from reality. He may believe he caused a death. He may believe he murdered someone, although he cannot say who or how. It is the auditor's task to recover the past failure in decision.

The partially obstructed case on the subject of future goals can be helped by the auditor.

IT IS NOT THE ROLE OF THE AUDITOR TO POSTULATE FOR THE PRECLEAR. POSTULATING BY THE AUDITOR RESULTS IN A MOMENTARY UPSURGE AND THEN A RELAPSE. ENCOURAGEMENT IS ROUTINE IN LIFE. IT'S NOT VERY THERAPEUTIC. DATA ON A NEW VIEWPOINT CAN HELP EVALUATION, BUT THIS IS THE ROLE OF A TEACHER.

Future goals take care of themselves when the preclear moves out into Beingness. The future is always full of traps. Where would we ever get randomity and adventure if it was not? It is a matter of facing the future, confident and unafraid despite obstacles, that distinguishes the superior being. The blunt question about "How (the preclear) actually feels about dying?" tests his condition. If he doesn't care, he is a fool. If he doesn't want it, but isn't afraid of it, he'll do.

$\mathcal{T}$HE
EMOTIONAL
CURVE

*"If the auditor must know anything backwards,
forwards, upside down, asleep or awake,
it is the Emotional Curve."*

$\mathcal{T}$HE
EMOTIONAL CURVE

F THE AUDITOR MUST know anything backwards, forwards, upside down, asleep or awake, it is the EMOTIONAL CURVE.

The auditor can neglect everything and anything on a case. He may even use a past -ology or indoctrinate his preclear into the worship of golden calves or professors. He can be pompous, idiotic or a Homo sapiens. So long as he understands, uses and reduces the emotional curve, he will succeed in accomplishing at least part of his mission.

Hence, attend!

THE EMOTIONAL CURVE IS THAT DROP OR RISE ON THE TONE SCALE ATTEND TO FAILURE TO CONTROL ON ANY DYNAMIC OR TO THE RECIPIENT OF AN ALLY ON ANY DYNAMIC.

The drop falls from above 2.5 down to Apathy in a steep curve. It occurs in seconds or minutes or hours. The speed of its fall is an index of the severity of the failure.

Death of an ally is received as a failure to keep the ally alive. This is followed by entering into the facsimiles of the ally and trying to jar him into life again, which is a second failure and which occludes the ally because the preclear is now living *as* the ally.

The emotional curve is a period with an exclamation point to the past. One's own death would be an emotional curve.

The flight down the emotional curve is as follows: State of Beingness, Antagonism against Not-Beingness, Fear of Not-Beingness, Grief about Not-Beingness, Acceptance of Not-Beingness.

These consecutive steps may be so swift that they jam into a blur which seemed to contain only a sudden shift from Beingness to Not-Beingness.

BEINGNESS is a supposed or actual control of the environment.

NOT-BEINGNESS is an acceptance of control by the environment and abdication even of control of self.

An early curve was: "I'll eat you." "I'm fighting you." "I'm losing." "I've lost. Eat me."

An earlier curve was: "I'm alive." "I'm wiped out by MEST and therefore I'm MEST."

The curve is addressed for this lifetime. It is located by getting the preclear to recall a time when he was happy and suddenly was made sad. He is then persuaded to re-experience this curve as emotion. He is run through that incident until it is desensitized (which may be at once or after several runs). Another such curve is located. One after another, curve incidents are taken from the case.

Suddenly or gradually, the SERVICE FACSIMILE CHAIN is in view and is run, one incident or another, until a whole service facsimile reduces. Then other service facsimiles of the chain are run until the preclear is clearly in possession of his own ability to postulate at will on his health or state.

Running the emotional curve will get the preclear into Grief discharges, Fear discharges or Anger discharges. These can be run, verbalized or not verbalized, over and over, as emotion.

The auditor should prepare to be extremely thorough about the emotional curve.

Running the curve in reverse locates the false supports and identities the preclear has assumed. This is done by finding a time when the preclear was "sad" or apathetic and running up to a time when he was in control of his environment again. This recovers the "arrivals of the US Cavalry" (and has given false value to that cavalry). The preclear will not get rid of emotional attachments or even disclose allies unless the reverse curve is run. A preclear who has been lifted up by such supports, clings forever afterwards to those supports and fetishes which remind him of those supports.

A typical reverse curve: Disobedience, punishment begun, intervention of Grandma. Bawl out by non-com, rescue by officer. News of possible death, cancellation of news by word of survival.

When the emotional curve went down, the preclear considered himself dead and his own past occluded. When the emotional curve went up, the preclear considered himself part of the identity of the rescuer.

WE WANT THE PRECLEAR AS A NEW SELF-DETERMINED SELF.

When the preclear is advanced to the Ninth Act, the running of emotional curves is fast and simple. The preclear fairly flies into higher and higher self-possession.

When the running of emotional curves is concluded, the preclear should be well advanced toward being in valence and not caring whether he is or not. Perceptics should be on.

It should be noted that the rising curve follows the down curve, when the rising curve exists.

A service facsimile is a down emotional curve, a counterfeit dying and a resurrection on a rising curve.

AN
ANALYSIS OF
SELF-DETERMINISM

*"One is Faith. The source, content of
and contact with Faith is You."*

AN ANALYSIS OF SELF-DETERMINISM

*T*HE GOAL of the auditor with his preclear is *not* the release of a "psychosomatic," *not* the improvement of appearance, *not* greater efficiency or better interpersonal relations. These are incidental.

THE GOAL OF THE AUDITOR WITH THE PRECLEAR IS THE REHABILITATION OF THE PRECLEAR'S SELF-DETERMINISM.

In order to understand this goal, let us examine some data and have a *thorough* understanding of what self-determinism is. Before this science, there were vague pushes in that direction. But the state itself lacked definition and there was definitely no bridge built to it.

SELF-DETERMINISM is that state of being wherein the individual can or cannot be controlled by his environment according to his own choice. In that state, the individual has self-confidence in his control of the material universe and the organisms within it along every dynamic. He is confident about any and all abilities or talents he may possess. He is confident in his interpersonal relationships. He reasons, but does not need to react.

Full Self-Determinism along every dynamic is found at 20.0. A complete Other-Determined individual is at 0.0. A gradient scale lies between.

On the Tone Scale we have at the optimum level, I Am, at the lowest level, I Am Not. Between we have, from the optimum level down, varying degrees of I Am and I Am Not. The lower one goes, the more I Am Not there is and the less I Am. Here is the graph of the State of Beingness and the State of Not-Beingness. This is a range from 20.0 down to 0.0. Not-Beingness is Death.

There is a parallel column on the Tone Scale to the I Am, I Am Not gradient scale. This is the I Know, I Know Not scale. I Know is at 20.0. I Know Not is at 0.0. Between these lie, as one descends, I Understand, I Am Trying to Understand, I Will Not Understand, I Am Afraid to Understand, I Cannot Understand, I Know Not.

Another parallel scale would be I Have Trust at 20.0 and I Trust Nothing at 0.0. As one descends, one reaches less and less Trust and more and more Distrust, until we have Death.

The mystic, for millennia, has been talking about Faith. He never built a bridge to it. He made a terrible fundamental error in converting Faith to Have Faith. When he said Have Faith, he invited understanding, then confusion of understanding because one does *not* understand Faith. One *is* Faith.

The source, content of and contact with FAITH is YOU.

The result of this mystic error (and it is a very gross error) was to place individuals so far down the Tone Scale that "love" and propitiation became bywords and hocus-pocus and the order of the day. Here is a 1.1 religion. It is afraid to understand because it has to Have Faith, but it isn't Faith because Faith is not understanding. Hence, the general confusion at 1.1.

A byproduct of this is the fact that individuals who thus Have Faith are running too slow. You get ESP, hypnotism, mixed-up facsimiles with others, martyrdom, physical illness and all manner of unwanted things at this slow speed. It is too close to the static of Death at 0.0 and its people are awfully dead, ineffective and irrational.

People who are trying to Have Faith *aren't* Faith. Thus they Fear (1.1) and Propitiate (1.1) and are generally confused. One will not buy unreason at 20.0. They began by Knowing Faith and then became confused by having Faith explained.

Because of spectacular successes (rare as rarity), the mystic continued to strive for something he already had because he had no way to get back to where he was. The enormously successful points of Being Faith, in the sea of unsuccessful Having Faith, kept the mystic striving. It is possible now to achieve Faith, or regain what one has lost.

I Am, Faith, I Know are at 20.0 on up. At 20.0 on the gradient scale, they are at optimum unity with MEST (the physical universe). But as they rise from 20.0, they become less and less effective on MEST until top static is reached at 40.0. The scale is a circle. 40.0 and 0.0 are the same, so it is possible to go two ways toward Death. One is less well off at 21.0 than he is at 20.0, since the MEST is dwindling away. The austere but spindly and weak mystic who dwells upon abstracts is less able to Know.

There is an entire scale above 20.0 which matches the scale below 20.0 in undesirability. The organism slows down above 20.0. The static is thoroughly unobtainable with one's body, evidently, for the static at the top, in a pure state (40.0), is for one thing a –270°C. A person who relaxes to "not being in body" is at first assailed by counter-efforts and then begins to chill.

The various phenomena of mysticism are, in the main, explained by this scale. When one forsakes individuality on the way up, he of course can commingle with thoughts and other individualities. When he slows down below toward 0.0, he is again getting confused in his individuality, shifts valences easily, is hypnotic and is in a generally undesirable condition.

Another prime error has been made (and is part of our culture, both religious and scientific) and that is the error of "single source." At 1.1, single source looks to be the case. Also at 39.0. At neither point, however, is there any clear view. All life forms are *not* from a single source. The ideas of Nirvana, Valhalla, Adam, the original cell—each is now rather completely disproven. There is a source for every genetic line. By this is meant both a theta (thought static) and MEST form. There are as many sources as there are living organisms, each line distinct and individual. The similarity of form in a species is due to similar environments and age of the class, not single source. A positive proof lies in the finding that health, sanity and effectiveness exist where the greatest self-determinism can be rehabilitated. A negative proof is that, if it were single source, the discovery of the genetic line facsimiles (the blueprint of the body) should permit just one individual to go back and clear the original upsets for the whole human race. It has been tried several times. It affects none but the preclear. His source is the very model of self-determinism.

What then are you trying to do with your preclear?

You are rehabilitating him from a state of partially I Am Not to I Am, from I Know Not to I Know, from Distrust to Trust.

If you only concentrated upon Distrust in others of him and his Distrust of others, his enforced Faiths on others and the enforced

Faith of others on him, and with his Trust and Distrust on all dynamics, particularly self, and desensitized such facsimiles, your preclears would be at around 10.0 at least.

OCCLUDED CASES MAY BE ONLY BROKEN TRUST CASES. FOR THE PRECLEAR CANNOT TRUST HIMSELF, THUS CANNOT TRUST HIS RECALLS. RUN "TRUST–DISTRUST," AND ENFORCED AND BROKEN "I KNOW" AND "I AM" AND "FAITH" IN ACT FOUR.

RESPONSIBILITY

"Assumption of Full Responsibility is a statement of control of the environment and persons within it without necessity of control."

RESPONSIBILITY

I N THE Fourteenth Act, the proper CONTROL CENTER is rehabilitated.

This is done by an indoctrination of the principles of RESPONSIBILITY and the running of RESPONSIBILITY.

An auditor, thus, must understand this subject thoroughly. The preclear will make his largest leap ahead with the Fourteenth Act.

DEFINITION: RESPONSIBILITY IS THE ABILITY AND WILLINGNESS TO ASSUME THE STATUS OF FULL SOURCE AND CAUSE FOR ALL EFFORTS AND COUNTER-EFFORTS ON ALL DYNAMICS.

There is no compromise with Full Responsibility. It lies above 20.0 on the Tone Scale and is descended from in order to effect randomity, but is descended from with the full knowledge of its assumption. It means responsibility for all acts, all emotions on every dynamic and in every sphere as one's own. It includes such "disrelated" data as the death of an individual one has never met on a highway on which one has never traveled at the hands of a stranger, no matter how culpable. One does not "send to find for whom the bell tolls" without full willingness to have tolled it and to have caused the cause of its tolling.

There is a Scale of Responsibility between Full Responsibility and Full Other-Responsibility, where the former is above 20.0 and the latter is at 0.0. Complete negation of responsibility is complete admission of being under the complete control of the environment. Assumption of Full Responsibility is a statement of control of the environment and persons within it without necessity of control.

There is a cycle of responsibility. One acts and seeks to negate his responsibility for such action by placing the "reason" at another's door. This works so long as one succeeds in making another accept responsibility for the action. The moment this action fails and another does not accept it, the entire action comes back at one. It is then a matter of fault and fixed (by another) blame and stirs the emotion of "guilt." Before this cycle begins, there is no aberration, no matter *what* has been done, no matter *what* has happened to anyone. The action occurs, but is no cause for discussion or justice until one seeks to shunt cause elsewhere than self. This starts the cycle and eventually comes back as "fault." Full Responsibility is not *fault*, it is recognition of being *cause*.

RATIONALIZATION is wholly an attempt to shunt responsibility. Whatever occurs to one, wherever on whatever track, is actually on his own responsibility (as the student will realize as soon as he re-evaluates the factors involved and as soon as he sees the enormous effect of this process).

The highest common denominator so far reached on occlusion is the responsibility factor. One is occluded on whatever he has tried not to be responsible for. He refuses responsibility for the incident, thus he has no control or responsibility for the facsimile of the incident. One can control nothing without assuming Full Responsibility for it.

Let us survey fundamentals.

Self-Determinism, Self-Confidence, I Know, I Am lie along 20.0. All knowledge is known at source, as witness the theta manufacture of complex compounds not yet touchable by chemists. One thus, by extrapolation, did not *agree* to survive. One had a *free choice* to survive, quite obviously.

The "agree" viewpoint is occasioned by postulating obedience to the Supreme Being, which postulate is demonstrably not workable as it poses a low-scale point for the Eighth Dynamic which would drag down all the other dynamics at once to zero and would continue them there and life would become impossible. Notwithstanding this point, which may or may not be acceptable, there are points which are inexorable.

Overall life, through all, tracks in a continuous survival through many "deaths." Succumb is only relative. Total succumb would be a discontinuance of the theta line, which demonstrably has not happened in any line on Earth today and which, by extrapolation and by the nature of the Life Static, will not happen tomorrow—for only MEST has time. Theta changes the organism form by varying efforts and counter-efforts and natural selection and planned development in MEST.

Development or even rationalization (negation of responsibility establishing conflict for development) establish randomity. And randomity is apparently vital in order to effect a conquest of MEST (our closest approach to *why* SURVIVAL!—being a conquest of the material universe by theta).

One is obviously conceived after free choice.

One obviously seeks and selects randomity on free choice.

Every individual is possessed of an urge for survival on every one of the eight dynamics. He can exercise free choice for the survival of every one of the eight. Indeed, since he has existed prior to any existing situation, he had the free choice to do something about it and thus had free choice about any existing situation. At least the problem resolves itself in this fashion. Its proof is that preclears soar up the Tone Scale on acceptance of Full Responsibility and the proposition is thus credited by its workability.

Running back any happenstance, *before* the cycle of blame-failure-guilt is started, will discover that the preclear had Full Responsibility for anything done to him or by him or, reaching far back, for anything done to anybody by anything or anybody. Full Responsibility for AAs occurs, if only in choosing conception. Anyone alive today had responsibility in creating our social order.

A soldier shot on the field of a battle may "blame" the sniper, the Selective Service, the stupidity of government. *But* he nevertheless had Full Responsibility not only for being there and getting shot, but for the sniper, Selective Service and the stupidity of government.

You may locate any RATIONALIZATION CYCLE merely by finding any mis-emotion such as Antagonism, Anger, Fear, Grief or Apathy on the part of the preclear for anything or anybody. You will find then a cycle wherein the preclear considered himself affected by environment, blamed environment (and environment contains all dynamics including self), failed to make the blame stick and received the consequences, thus losing self-determinism, thus getting controlled by environment, thus getting aberrated, thus getting and using the service facsimile.

The auditor is not seeking the point where the preclear accepts the harm which came to him as his *fault.* The auditor is seeking the point where the preclear decided it was not his responsibility and then the earlier point of refusal of responsibility. Get the *fault-acceptance* point and you will find Apathy, since here is agreement with accusation—wrong point. Get the first instant of rationalization and then the earlier generalization of negated responsibility and you will find the postulates which deny Full Responsibility.

A postulate of "illness so as not to attend school" is not the primary postulate on the chain. The primary postulate on this chain is "refusal of Full Responsibility for school."

OCCLUSIONS are resolved by Full Responsibility on the subject. This includes occluded persons.

DUB-IN is resolved by a Full Responsibility resolution, for the dub-in is far more active in rationalization than an occluded case.

The preclear—understanding all this—may yet wonder when he discovers in his past a person who avowedly has "Full Responsibility," is "always right," and yet made him unhappy. Let the preclear look in this person for the actuality of Full Responsibility and the person in question will be found to have suspicions, antagonisms and rationalizations and is thus discovered to be lacking in Full Responsibility after all.

The environment starts to control the individual the moment he rationalizes away his inherent Full Responsibility. The individual becomes "unable" to handle any facsimile of any incident for which he has not assumed Full Responsibility, thus becomes subject to facsimiles "handling" him.

Attempting to invalidate someone is attempting to negate Full Responsibility for that person. The person who insists it is "your fault" is invalidated, on a low-tone level, by insisting it is not your fault. Thus, assuming "fault" seems to validate the accusation of the person so claiming. Assumption of Full Responsibility is also assumption of the accusative person as a responsibility.

For definition, the Responsibility Scale drops to its next level, I Am Responsible and I Must Do Something About It. This dwindles down through I Won't Be Responsible, I Am Afraid of Responsibility For It, I Don't Care, It's No Use Being Responsible. The lowest rung is No Responsibility For Anything.

Past deaths are occluded because one does not take their responsibility, such deaths being contrary, on a shallow level in an aberrated society, to Survive. Thus, past deaths are sometimes hard to explain to people, for they would not have any responsibility on their own and therefore refuse it on the subject.

Using symbols for actuality is negating responsibility.

Several group experiments, including teaching every man on a naval vessel that he was responsible for everything, have been made which validated these postulates. A negative series was also made with opposite results, again demonstrating these postulates.

How irresponsible can one be? Refusal of Full Responsibility for dying and its Survival value.

FULL RESPONSIBILITY

Cause and Effect

"Cause is the Life Static itself."

*F*ULL RESPONSIBILITY
Cause and Effect

N INDIVIDUAL IS evidently designed to be CAUSE.

When one speaks of RESPONSIBILITY, he means the determination of the CAUSE which produced the EFFECT.

THE GOAL OF FULL RESPONSIBILITY IS NOT ATTAINED SIMPLY BY MAKING A NEW POSTULATE. IT IS ATTAINED BY DISCOVERING AND REDUCING THE PRECLEAR'S ASSIGNMENT OF CAUSE.

Ordinarily people call the assignment of cause "blame."

If one assigns cause to something, he delivers to that entity power. This is not mystical. It is a new discovery of hitherto unknown phenomena. By its understanding and use, strange visios and occlusions resolve.

A swift survey of emotions demonstrates that a gradient scale from Cause drops down to Effect.

Cause is the Life Static itself.

Full Effect would be MEST, or a dead body.

An organism seeks to be Cause without becoming Effect.

Cause is above 20.0.

Effect is at 0.0.

The gradient scale goes downward in this wise: One is Cause. He begins motion and is able to change it. He is committed to motion and becomes less able to change it. He comes into a range of being the effect of motion. He seeks to hold motion to keep from being an effect at 1.5. He is unable to hold motion and begins to fear motion at 1.1, propitiating it. He regrets anything about motion and is in Grief, as an effect, at 0.5. He becomes and recognizes that he has become Effect at 0.1.

A strange visio on a case will vanish if regret is scanned up from it. Occlusions will turn on if blame is scanned off the occluded object or person, including self.

This operates on any of the eight dynamics. That which one blames becomes a power and is occluded as unexaminable, including self. That which is in stationary visio is that which one regrets having caused.

There is a cycle on any chain on any dynamic as follows: One causes something. He fails. He postulates blame (1.5). He establishes sympathy and regrets. Each new blame thrusts him further, on that chain, into an Apathy. Find a thing on any dynamic (including the First Dynamic) which one blames and the auditor will discover, at the bottom of the chain, a cause and failure of magnitude. He need only scan blame and regret from the chain to recover the basic incident. Then he should exhaust from that incident its emotional curve. This recovers any computation on a case.

Effort can be run on Cause and Effect, but the Effect of course is Apathy and should probably be run as counter-effort.

FULL RESPONSIBILITY RESOLVES ONLY IN THIS WISE.

A SUMMARY OF ADVANCED PROCEDURE

"Go through each successive step
with ease again."

A SUMMARY OF ADVANCED PROCEDURE

Act One—Auditor rehabilitates any lack of real desire to give preclear complete ownership of preclear. POSTULATES, FULL RESPONSIBILITY.

Act Two—Auditor establishes preclear's confusions about auditor identity. MIMICRY, ARC, MIS-ASSOCIATIONS BY PRECLEAR, POSTULATES.

Act Three—Auditor rehabilitates preclear's confusions about present time facsimiles and actualities. ARC, VALIDATION MEST, POSTULATES.

Act Four—Accessibility of preclear with preclear. PAST, PRESENT AND FUTURE. GOALS. TRUST–DISTRUST. POSTULATES.

Act Five—ASSESSMENT. Evaluation without processing as such.

Act Six—Location of and identification of SERVICE FACSIMILE. AGE FLASHES. EXAMINATION OF DRAMATIZATIONS. WHAT PRECLEAR DOES TO OTHERS. Establish without auditor evaluation that service facsimile exists.

Act Seven—Establishment of CONTROL CENTER, whether right or wrong. STRAIGHTWIRE ON EFFORTS BY OTHERS TO SHIFT CENTER. AGREEMENTS TO CHANGE HABITS. PRECLEAR'S EFFORTS TO CHANGE OTHERS.

Act Eight—Devaluation of language with START, STOP, CHANGE STRAIGHTWIRE, WITH ATTENTION TO MOVE. STRAIGHTWIRE. LOCK SCANNING IF PRECLEAR NOW ABOVE 2.0. MEST PROCESSING OF ENTHETA. Essentially orientation of preclear in MEST UNIVERSE.

Act Nine—Running EMOTIONAL CURVES. EMOTIONAL CURVE PROCESSES. RUNNING EMOTIONAL LOCKS OVER AGAIN AND AGAIN.

Act Ten—Running out or desensitizing the SERVICE FACSIMILE. THOUGHT, EFFORT, EMOTION. IF NOT DONE EASILY IN THREE HOURS, GO TO NEXT ACT.

Act Eleven—All SYMPATHY on every dynamic. EMOTIONAL CURVES. SYMPATHY. RUN AS INDIVIDUAL LOCKS. THEN LOCK SCAN. ALL DYNAMICS, CURRENT LIFETIME.

Act Twelve—All EMOTION, all dynamics. LOCK SCANNING except heavy incidents of secondary magnitude which are run as secondaries (HEAVY LOCKS, OVER AND OVER BY THEMSELVES AS INCIDENTS). FIVE HOURS MAXIMUM AUDITING TIME, whether out or not, go to next step.

Act Thirteen—Current lifetime, attempt to clear case of all POSTULATES and EVALUATIONS in current lifetime. THOUGHT. STRAIGHTWIRE. LOCK SCANNING. COMPUTATIONS.

Act Fourteen—Rehabilitate proper CONTROL CENTER. Requires instructing and orienting preclear. FULL RESPONSIBILITY.

Act Fifteen—Recheck case. GO THROUGH EACH SUCCESSIVE STEP WITH CASE AGAIN.

NOTE: This process for any case. Time allowance not completely determined for auditors at this writing. Estimated at ten hours actual auditing by auditor, plus fifty hours by preclear on self-help book.[*] Additional auditor time allowance on first four Acts for psychotics.

[*]Handbook for Preclears.

Advanced Procedure and Axioms

LRH GLOSSARY

"Act: A stage of processing. Applies solely to the particular process in use at a certain case level."

Advanced Procedure and Axioms
LRH GLOSSARY

*(These words are listed in the order in which they appear
in the chapter ADVANCED PROCEDURE.)*

ACT:

A stage of processing. Applies solely to the particular process
in use at a certain case level.

FIFTEEN:

(noun) A designation to denote a finished case. Solely for case
recording to designate a case advanced to current completion.
This is a Foundation number system for preclears. A case
is noted on record by the Act number to which it has been
advanced.

AUDITOR:

One who listens and computes. A technician of this science.

PRECLEAR:

One who has entered processing en route to becoming a Fifteen.

CLEAR:

(verb) The act of desensitizing or releasing a thought impression or a series of impressions or observations in the past or a postulate or an emotion or an effort or an entire facsimile. The preclear either releases his hold on the facsimile (memory) or the facsimile itself is desensitized. The word is taken from electronic computers or common office adding machines and describes an action similar to clearing past computations from the machines.

CLEAR:

(noun) A much misunderstood state of being. The word has been used before with other meanings. It has been mistaken as an absolute. It is still used. It is used here as electronics slang and can apply to a chain, an incident or a computation.

CENTER OF CONTROL:

The awareness of awareness unit of the mind. This is not part of the brain, but part of the mind, the brain being physiological. The mind has two control centers possible, by definition, the right and the left. One is an actual genetic control center. The other is a sub-control center, subservient to the control center.

STRAIGHTWIRE:

A process of recalling from present time, with some perception or at least a concept, a past incident. The name Straightwire derives from the MEST communications process of connecting two points of a communications system. It is essentially memory work. It is applied to postulates, evaluations, incidents, scenes, emotions, or any data which may be in the storage banks of the mind without "sending the preclear" into the incident itself. It is done with the preclear sitting up, eyes open or shut. The auditor is very alert. Straightwire is done rapidly. The preclear is not permitted to wander or reminisce. He responds to questions on the part of the auditor. MANY PRECLEARS DISLIKE BEING QUESTIONED. THE AUDITOR MUST THEN FIRST RESOLVE THE POSTULATES AGAINST BEING QUESTIONED. This would be called "Clearing for Broad Straightwire."

POSTULATE:

(verb) To conclude, decide or resolve a problem or to set a pattern for the future or to nullify a pattern of the past.

POSTULATE:

(noun) A conclusion, decision or resolution made by the individual himself on his own self-determinism on data of the past, known or unknown. The postulate is always known. It is made upon the evaluation of data by the individual or on impulse without data. It resolves a problem of the past, decides on problems or observations in the present or sets a pattern for the future.

PAST POSTULATES:

Decisions or conclusions the preclear has made in the past and to which he is still subjected in the present. Past postulates are uniformly invalid since they cannot resolve present environment.

FACSIMILES:

A facsimile is a memory recording for a finite period of time. It is considered that memory is a static without wavelength, weight, mass or position in space (in other words, a true static) which yet receives the impression of time, space, energy and matter. A careful examination of the phenomena of thought and the behavior of the human mind leads one to this conclusion. The conclusion is itself a postulate, used because it is extremely useful and workable. This is a point of echelon in research that a facsimile can be so described. The description is mathematical and an abstract and may or may not be actual. When a thought recording is so regarded, the problems of the mind rapidly resolve. Facsimiles are said to be "stored." They act upon the physical universe switchboard, called the brain and nervous and glandular system, to monitor action. They appear to have motion and weight only because motion and weight are recorded into them. They are not stored in the cells. They impinge upon the cells. Proof of this matter rests in the fact that an energy which became a facsimile a long time ago can be recontacted and is found to be violent on the contact. Pain is stored as a facsimile. Old pain can be recontacted. Old pain in facsimile form, old emotion in facsimile form, can reimpose itself on present time in such a wise as to deform or otherwise physically effect the body. You can go back to the last time you hurt yourself and find there and re-experience the pain of that hurt unless you are very occluded. You can recover efforts and exertions you have made or which have been made against you in the past. Yet the cells themselves, which have finite life, are long since replaced although the body goes on. Hence, the facsimile theory. The word facsimile is used, as bluntly as one uses it, in connection with a drawing of a box top instead of the actual box top. It means a similar article rather than the article itself. You can recall a memory picture of an elephant or a photograph. The elephant and the photograph are no longer present. A facsimile of them is stored in your mind. A facsimile is complete with every perception of the environment present when that facsimile was made, including sight, sound, smell, taste, weight, joint position and so on through half a hundred perceptions. Just because you cannot recall motion or these perceptions does not mean they were not recorded fully and in motion with every perception channel you had at the time. It does mean that you have interposed a stop between the facsimile and the recall mechanisms of your control centers. There are facsimiles of everything you have experienced in your entire lifetime and everything you have imagined.

Heavy Facsimile:

A heavy facsimile used to be known as an "engram." In view of the fact that it has been found to be stored elsewhere than in the cells, the term "heavy facsimile" has now come into use. A heavy facsimile is an experience, complete with all perceptions and emotions and thoughts and efforts, occupying a precise place in space and a moment in time. It can be an operation, an injury, a term of heavy physical exertion or even a death. It is composed of the preclear's own effort and the effort of the environment (counter-effort).

Environment:

The surroundings of the preclear from moment to moment, in particular or in general, including people, pets, mechanical objects, weather, culture, clothing or the Supreme Being. Anything he perceives or believes he perceives.

The objective environment is the environment everyone agrees is there. The subjective environment is the environment the individual himself believes is there. They may not agree.

ACCESSIBILITY:

The state of being willing to be processed (technical sense in this science). The state of being willing to have interpersonal relations (social sense). For the individual himself, accessibility with self means whether or not an individual can recontact his past experiences or data. A man with a "bad memory" (interposed blocks between control center and facsimiles) has memories which are not accessible to him.

PSYCHOTIC:

An individual who is out of contact to a thorough extent with his present time environment and who does not compute into the future. He may be an acute psychotic, wherein he becomes psychotic for only a few minutes at a time and only occasionally in certain environments (as in rages or apathies), or he may be a chronic psychotic (or in a continual disconnect with the future and present). Psychotics who are dramatically harmful to others are considered dangerous enough to be put away. Psychotics who are harmful on a less dramatic basis are no less harmful to their environment and are no less psychotic.

COMPUTING PSYCHOTIC:

One who is running on a circuit, a circuit being a pseudo-personality out of a facsimile strong enough to dictate to the individual and BE the individual.

Dramatizing Psychotic:

One who dramatizes one type of facsimile only.

Broken:

Slang used in the wise of "breaking a case," meaning that one breaks the hold of the preclear on a non-survival facsimile. Used in greater or lesser magnitude, such as "breaking a circuit" or "breaking into a chain" or "breaking a computation." Never breaking the preclear or his spirit, but breaking what is breaking the preclear.

Assists:

The straight perception-by-perception running, over and over, of an accident or incident, until it is desensitized as a facsimile and cannot affect the preclear. The assist is used immediately after accidents or operations. It takes away shock and most of the harmful effects of the incident and promotes healing. It is done by starting the individual at the beginning of the incident, with the first awareness of the incident, just as though the preclear were living it all the way through again with full perception of sight, sound, etc., as nearly as they can be obtained. An assist run, for instance, immediately after a dental operation takes all the shock out of the operation. One concludes an assist by picking up the auditing as another incident and running through the auditing and the decision to be audited. An assist saves lives and materially speeds healing.

Recovery:

Recovery of one's own ability to determine one's existence.

ASSESSMENT:

An inventory, an examination or a calculation or evaluation of a case.

THOUGHT:

The facsimiles one has recorded of his various environments and the facsimiles he has created with his imaginings, their recombination and evaluations and conclusions, for the purpose of determining action or no action or potential action or no action. Thought is used also to mean a process treating awareness level recordings, as distinct from non-awareness level recordings.

EMOTION:

The catalyst used by the control center to monitor physical action. The relay system, via glands, interposed between "I" and self and, by thought, others. The main emotions are Happiness in which one has confidence and enjoyment in his goals and a belief in his control of environment; Boredom in which one has lost confidence and direction but is not defeated; Antagonism wherein one feels his control threatened; Anger wherein one seeks to destroy that which threatens and seeks without good direction beyond destruction; Covert Hostility wherein one seeks to destroy while reassuring his target that he is not so seeking; Fear wherein one is catalyzed to flee; Grief in which one recognizes loss; Apathy in which one accepts failure on all dynamics and pretends Death. Other emotions are a volume or lack of volume of those named. Shame or Embarrassment are emotions peculiar to groups or interpersonal relations and are on a level with Grief, denoting loss of position in a group. Emotion is the glandular system

---

parallel of motion and each emotion reflects action to gain or lose motion. At a high level, one is sending back motion; at a mid level, one is holding motion; at a lower level, motion is sweeping through and over one.

Psychosomatic Illness:

A term used in common parlance to denote a condition "resulting from a state of mind." Such illnesses account for about 70 percent of all ills, by popular report. Technically, in this science, "a chronic or continuing painful facsimile to which the preclear is holding to account for failures." Arthritis, bursitis, tendonitis, myopia, astigmatism, bizarre aches and pains, sinusitis, colds, ulcers, migraine headaches, toothache, poliomyelitis deformities, fatness, skin malformations, etc., etc., etc., etc., are a few of these legion of chronic somatics. They are traceable to service facsimiles.

Repetitive Straightwire:

Attention called to an incident over and over, amongst other incidents, until it is desensitized. Used on conclusions or incidents which do not easily surrender.

Lock Scanning:

A process which starts the preclear from a point in the past, with which he has made solid contact, up through all similar incidents, without verbalization. This is done over and over, each time trying to start at an earlier incident of the same kind, until the preclear extroverts on the subject of the chain. "Boil-off" often results, wherein the preclear seems to go to sleep. Avoid boil-off, for it is not therapeutic and will eventually result in reduced tone.

Boil-off is a lazy auditor's excuse to be idle and facsimiles are in such severe conflict that they will not resolve without resolving postulates first.

Lock Scanning is a standardized drill, started on signal and ended with the preclear saying he is again in present time. It can be done on any subject. ABOVE 2.0 only.

SERVICE FACSIMILE:

A definitely non-survival situation contained in a facsimile which is called into action by the individual to explain his failures. A service facsimile may be one of an illness, an injury, an inability. The facsimile begins with a down emotional curve and ends with an upward emotional curve. Between these it has pain. A service facsimile *is* the pattern which is the chronic "psychosomatic illness." It may contain coughs, fever, aches, rashes, any manifestation of a non-survival character, mental or physical. It may even be a suicide effort. It is complete with all perceptions. It has many similar facsimiles. It has many locks. The possession and use of a service facsimile distinguishes a Homo sapiens.

A service facsimile is that facsimile which the preclear uses to apologize for his failures. In other words, it is used to make others wrong and procure their cooperation in the survival of the preclear.

SERVICE FACSIMILE CHAIN:

The entire chain of similar incidents which comprise the total repertoire of the individual who is explaining his failure and thus seeking support.

RELEASE:

(verb) The act of taking the perceptions or effort or effectiveness out of a heavy facsimile, or taking away the preclear's hold on the facsimile.

EFFORT:

The physical-force manifestation of motion. A sharp effort against an individual produces pain. A strenuous effort produces discomfort. Effort can be recalled and re-experienced by the preclear. No preclear below 2.0 should be called upon to use effort as such, as he is incapable of handling it and will stick in it. The essential part of a painful facsimile is its effort, not its perceptions.

COUNTER-EFFORT:

The individual's own effort is simply called EFFORT. The efforts of the environment are called COUNTER-EFFORTS.

EFFORT PROCESSING:

Effort Processing is done by running moments of physical stress. These are run either as simple efforts or counter-efforts or as whole precise incidents. Such incidents as those which contain physical pain or heavy stress of motion (such as injuries, accidents or illnesses) are addressed by Effort Processing.

GENETIC:

By line of protoplasm and by facsimiles and by MEST forms, the individual has arrived in the present age from a past beginning. Genetic applies to the protoplasm line of father and mother to child, grown child to new child and so forth.

EMOTIONAL CURVE:

The drop from any position (on the Tone Scale) above 2.0 to a position below 2.0 on the realization of failure or inadequacy. It is easily recovered by preclears.

SYMPATHY:

The posing of an emotional state similar to the emotional state of an individual in Grief or Apathy.

DYNAMICS:

The central drives of an individual. They are numbered from one to eight as follows: (1) Self survival; (2) Survival through children (includes sexual act); (3) Survival by groups including social and political as well as commercial; (4) Survival through Mankind as a whole; (5) Survival through Life including any species, vegetable or animal; (6) Survival through MEST; (7) Survival through theta or the static itself; (8) (Written as infinity—∞) Survival through a Supreme Being. Each individual is surviving for all eight.

THETA:

The mathematical symbol— θ —for the static of thought. By theta is meant the static itself. By "facsimile" is meant theta which contains impressions by perception.

MEST:

A compound word made up of the first letters of MATTER, ENERGY, SPACE and TIME. A coined word for the PHYSICAL UNIVERSE.

THETA IS NOT CONSIDERED AS PART OF THE PHYSICAL UNIVERSE, BUT IS NOT CONSIDERED ABSOLUTELY AS NOT PART OF THE PHYSICAL UNIVERSE.

PERCEPTIONS:

By means of physical waves, rays and particles of the physical universe, impressions of the environment enter through the "sense channels," such as the eyes and optic nerves, the nose and olfactory nerves, the ears and aural nerves, interbody nerves for interbody perceptions, etc., etc. These are all "perceptions" up to the instant they record as facsimiles, at which moment they become "recordings." When recalled they are perceptions again, being again entered into sense channels from the recall side. There are over half a hundred separate perceptions all being recorded at once.

TEN:

A case advanced to the point of released service facsimile.

DEFINITIONS, LOGICS AND AXIOMS

"A fundamental operation of theta in surviving is bringing order into the chaos of the physical universe."

DEFINITIONS, LOGICS AND AXIOMS

THESE ARE the Definitions, Logics and Axioms of this science. It should be borne in mind that these actually form epistemology, the science of knowledge. These cannot but embrace various fields and sciences. They are listed in this volume without further elucidation, but will be found to be self-explanatory for the most part. Adequate phenomena exist to demonstrate the self-evidence of these Definitions, Postulates, Logics and Axioms.

The first section, the Logics, is separate from the Axioms only in that from the system of thinking so evaluated, the Axioms themselves flow. The word "logics" is used here to mean postulates pertaining to the organizational structure of alignment.

THE LOGICS

LOGIC 1:

KNOWLEDGE IS A WHOLE GROUP OR SUBDIVISION OF A GROUP OF DATA OR SPECULATIONS OR CONCLUSIONS ON DATA OR METHODS OF GAINING DATA.

LOGIC 2:

A BODY OF KNOWLEDGE IS A BODY OF DATA, ALIGNED OR UNALIGNED, OR METHODS OF GAINING DATA.

LOGIC 3:

ANY KNOWLEDGE WHICH CAN BE SENSED, MEASURED OR EXPERIENCED BY ANY ENTITY IS CAPABLE OF INFLUENCING THAT ENTITY.

COROLLARY: THAT KNOWLEDGE WHICH CANNOT BE SENSED, MEASURED OR EXPERIENCED BY ANY ENTITY OR TYPE OF ENTITY CANNOT INFLUENCE THAT ENTITY OR TYPE OF ENTITY.

LOGIC 4:

A DATUM IS A FACSIMILE OF STATES OF BEING, STATES OF NOT BEING, ACTIONS OR INACTIONS, CONCLUSIONS OR SUPPOSITIONS IN THE PHYSICAL OR ANY OTHER UNIVERSE.

LOGIC 5:

A DEFINITION OF TERMS IS NECESSARY TO THE ALIGNMENT, STATEMENT AND RESOLUTION OF SUPPOSITIONS, OBSERVATIONS, PROBLEMS AND SOLUTIONS AND THEIR COMMUNICATION.

DEFINITION—DESCRIPTIVE DEFINITION: *One which classifies by characteristics, by describing existing states of being.*

DEFINITION—DIFFERENTIATIVE DEFINITION: *One which compares unlikeness to existing states of being or not being.*

DEFINITION—ASSOCIATIVE DEFINITION: *One which declares likeness to existing states of being or not being.*

DEFINITION—ACTION DEFINITION: *One which delineates cause and potential change of state of being by cause of existence, inexistence, action, inaction, purpose or lack of purpose.*

LOGIC 6:

ABSOLUTES ARE UNOBTAINABLE.

LOGIC 7:

GRADIENT SCALES ARE NECESSARY TO THE EVALUATION OF PROBLEMS AND THEIR DATA.

This is the tool of infinity-valued logic: Absolutes are unobtainable. Terms such as good and bad, alive and dead, right and wrong, are used only in conjunction with gradient scales. On the scale of right and wrong, everything above zero or center would be more and more right, approaching an infinite rightness, and everything below center would be more and more wrong, approaching infinite wrongness. All things assisting the survival of the survivor are considered to be *right* for the survivor. All things inhibiting survival from the viewpoint of the survivor can be considered *wrong* for the survivor. The more a thing assists survival, the more it can be considered right for the survivor; the more a thing or action inhibits survival, the more it is wrong from the viewpoint of the intended survivor.

COROLLARY: ANY DATUM HAS ONLY RELATIVE TRUTH.

COROLLARY: TRUTH IS RELATIVE TO ENVIRONMENTS, EXPERIENCE AND TRUTH.

LOGIC 8:

A DATUM CAN BE EVALUATED ONLY BY A DATUM OF COMPARABLE MAGNITUDE.

LOGIC 9:

A DATUM IS AS VALUABLE AS IT HAS BEEN EVALUATED.

LOGIC 10:

THE VALUE OF A DATUM IS ESTABLISHED BY THE AMOUNT OF ALIGNMENT (relationship) IT IMPARTS TO OTHER DATA.

LOGIC 11:

THE VALUE OF A DATUM OR FIELD OF DATA CAN BE ESTABLISHED BY ITS DEGREE OF ASSISTANCE IN SURVIVAL OR ITS INHIBITION TO SURVIVAL.

LOGIC 12:

THE VALUE OF A DATUM OR A FIELD OF DATA IS MODIFIED BY THE VIEWPOINT OF THE OBSERVER.

LOGIC 13:

PROBLEMS ARE RESOLVED BY COMPARTMENTING THEM INTO AREAS OF SIMILAR MAGNITUDE AND DATA, COMPARING THEM TO DATA ALREADY KNOWN OR PARTIALLY KNOWN, AND RESOLVING EACH AREA. DATA WHICH CANNOT BE KNOWN IMMEDIATELY MAY BE RESOLVED BY ADDRESSING WHAT IS KNOWN AND USING ITS SOLUTION TO RESOLVE THE REMAINDER.

LOGIC 14:

FACTORS INTRODUCED INTO A PROBLEM OR SOLUTION WHICH DO NOT DERIVE FROM NATURAL LAW BUT ONLY FROM AUTHORITARIAN COMMAND ABERRATE THAT PROBLEM OR SOLUTION.

LOGIC 15:

THE INTRODUCTION OF AN ARBITRARY INTO A PROBLEM OR SOLUTION INVITES THE FURTHER INTRODUCTION OF ARBITRARIES INTO PROBLEMS AND SOLUTIONS.

Logic 16:

An abstract postulate must be compared to the universe to which it applies and brought into the category of things which can be sensed, measured or experienced in that universe before such postulate can be considered workable.

Logic 17:

Those fields which most depend upon authoritative opinion for their data least contain known natural law.

Logic 18:

A postulate is as valuable as it is workable.

Logic 19:

The workability of a postulate is established by the degree to which it explains existing phenomena already known, by the degree that it predicts new phenomena which when looked for will be found to exist, and by the degree that it does not require that phenomena which do not exist in fact be called into existence for its explanation.

Logic 20:

A science may be considered to be a large body of aligned data which has similarity in application and which has been deduced or induced from basic postulates.

Logic 21:

Mathematics are methods of postulating or resolving real or abstract data in any universe and integrating by symbolization of data, postulates and resolutions.

LOGIC 22:

THE HUMAN MIND[*] IS AN OBSERVER, POSTULATOR, CREATOR AND STORAGE PLACE OF KNOWLEDGE.

LOGIC 23:

THE HUMAN MIND IS A SERVOMECHANISM TO ANY MATHEMATICS EVOLVED OR EMPLOYED BY THE HUMAN MIND.

POSTULATE: THE HUMAN MIND AND INVENTIONS OF THE HUMAN MIND ARE CAPABLE OF RESOLVING ANY AND ALL PROBLEMS WHICH CAN BE SENSED, MEASURED OR EXPERIENCED DIRECTLY OR INDIRECTLY.

COROLLARY: THE HUMAN MIND IS CAPABLE OF RESOLVING THE PROBLEM OF THE HUMAN MIND.

The borderline of solution of this science lies between *why* life is surviving and *how* life is surviving. It is possible to resolve *how* life is surviving without resolving *why* life is surviving.

LOGIC 24:

THE RESOLUTION OF THE PHILOSOPHICAL, SCIENTIFIC AND HUMAN STUDIES (such as economics, politics, sociology, medicine, criminology, etc.) DEPENDS PRIMARILY UPON THE RESOLUTION OF THE PROBLEMS OF THE HUMAN MIND.

The human mind by definition includes the awareness unit of the living organism, the observer, the computer of data, the spirit, the memory storage, the life force and the individual motivator of the living organism. It is used as distinct from the brain which can be considered to be motivated by the mind. —LRH

NOTE: The primary step in resolving the broad activities of Man could be considered to be the resolving of the activities of the mind itself. Hence, the Logics carry to this point and then proceed as Axioms concerning the human mind, such Axioms being substantiated as relative truths by much newly discovered phenomena. The ensuing Axioms, from Logic 24, apply no less to the various -ologies than they do to de-aberrating or improving the operation of the mind. It should not be thought that the following Axioms are devoted to the construction of anything as limited as a therapy, which is only incidental to the resolution of human aberration and such things as psychosomatic illnesses. These Axioms are capable of such solution, as has been demonstrated, but such a narrow application would indicate a very narrow scope of view.

AXIOMS

AXIOM 1:

THE SOURCE OF LIFE IS A STATIC OF PECULIAR AND PARTICULAR PROPERTIES.

AXIOM 2:

AT LEAST A PORTION OF THE STATIC CALLED LIFE IS IMPINGED UPON THE PHYSICAL UNIVERSE.

AXIOM 3:

THAT PORTION OF THE STATIC OF LIFE WHICH IS IMPINGED UPON THE PHYSICAL UNIVERSE HAS FOR ITS DYNAMIC GOAL, SURVIVAL AND ONLY SURVIVAL.

AXIOM 4:

THE PHYSICAL UNIVERSE IS REDUCIBLE TO MOTION OF ENERGY OPERATING IN SPACE THROUGH TIME.

AXIOM 5:

THAT PORTION OF THE STATIC OF LIFE CONCERNED WITH THE LIFE ORGANISMS OF THE PHYSICAL UNIVERSE IS CONCERNED WHOLLY WITH MOTION.

AXIOM 6:

THE LIFE STATIC HAS AS ONE OF ITS PROPERTIES THE ABILITY TO MOBILIZE AND ANIMATE MATTER INTO LIVING ORGANISMS.

AXIOM 7:

THE LIFE STATIC IS ENGAGED IN A CONQUEST OF THE PHYSICAL UNIVERSE.

Axiom 8:

The Life Static conquers the material universe by learning and applying the physical laws of the physical universe.

Symbol: The symbol for the *Life Static* in use hereafter is the Greek letter *theta* (θ).

Axiom 9:

A fundamental operation of *theta* in surviving is bringing order into the chaos of the physical universe.

Axiom 10:

Theta brings order into chaos by conquering whatever in *mest* may be pro-survival and destroying whatever in *mest* may be contra-survival, at least through the medium of life organisms.

Symbol: The symbol for the *physical universe* in use hereafter is *mest*, from the first letters of the words Matter, Energy, Space and Time, or the Greek letter *phi* (ϕ).

Axiom 11:

A life organism is composed of matter and energy in space and time, animated by *theta*.

Symbol: Living organism or organisms will hereafter be represented by the Greek letter *lambda* (λ).

Axiom 12:

The *mest* part of the organism follows the laws of the physical sciences. All *lambda* is concerned with motion.

AXIOM 13:

THETA OPERATING THROUGH *LAMBDA* CONVERTS THE FORCES OF THE PHYSICAL UNIVERSE INTO FORCES TO CONQUER THE PHYSICAL UNIVERSE.

AXIOM 14:

THETA WORKING UPON PHYSICAL UNIVERSE MOTION MUST MAINTAIN A HARMONIOUS RATE OF MOTION.

The limits of *lambda* are narrow, both as to thermal and mechanical motion.

AXIOM 15:

LAMBDA IS THE INTERMEDIATE STEP IN THE CONQUEST OF THE PHYSICAL UNIVERSE.

AXIOM 16:

THE BASIC FOOD OF ANY ORGANISM CONSISTS OF LIGHT AND CHEMICALS.

Organisms can exist only as higher levels of complexities because lower levels of converters exist.

Theta evolves organisms from lower to higher forms and supports them by the existence of lower converter forms.

AXIOM 17:

THETA, VIA *LAMBDA,* EFFECTS AN EVOLUTION OF *MEST.*

In this we have the waste products of organisms on the one hand as those very complex chemicals which bacteria make and, on the other hand, we have the physical face of the Earth being changed by animals and men, such changes as grass holding mountains from eroding or roots causing boulders to break, buildings being built, and rivers being dammed. There is obviously an evolution in *MEST* in progress under the incursion of *theta*.

AXIOM 18:

LAMBDA, EVEN WITHIN A SPECIES, VARIES IN ITS ENDOWMENT OF *THETA*.

AXIOM 19:

THE EFFORT OF *LAMBDA* IS TOWARD SURVIVAL.

THE GOAL OF *LAMBDA* IS SURVIVAL.

THE PENALTY OF FAILURE TO ADVANCE TOWARD THAT GOAL IS TO SUCCUMB.

> DEFINITION: *Persistence is the ability to exert continuance of effort toward survival goals.*

AXIOM 20:

LAMBDA CREATES, CONSERVES, MAINTAINS, ACQUIRES, DESTROYS, CHANGES, OCCUPIES, GROUPS AND DISPERSES *MEST. LAMBDA* SURVIVES BY ANIMATING AND MOBILIZING OR DESTROYING MATTER AND ENERGY IN SPACE AND TIME.

AXIOM 21:

LAMBDA IS DEPENDENT UPON OPTIMUM MOTION. MOTION WHICH IS TOO SWIFT AND MOTION WHICH IS TOO SLOW ARE EQUALLY CONTRA-SURVIVAL.

AXIOM 22:

THETA AND THOUGHT ARE SIMILAR ORDERS OF STATIC.

AXIOM 23:

ALL THOUGHT IS CONCERNED WITH MOTION.

AXIOM 24:

THE ESTABLISHMENT OF AN OPTIMUM MOTION IS A BASIC GOAL OF REASON.

> DEFINITION: Lambda *is a chemical heat engine existing in space and time motivated by the Life Static and directed by thought.*

171

AXIOM 25:

THE BASIC PURPOSE OF REASON IS THE CALCULATION OR ESTIMATION OF EFFORT.

AXIOM 26:

THOUGHT IS ACCOMPLISHED BY *THETA FACSIMILES* OF PHYSICAL UNIVERSE, ENTITIES OR ACTIONS.

AXIOM 27:

THETA IS SATISFIED ONLY WITH HARMONIOUS ACTION OR OPTIMUM MOTION AND REJECTS OR DESTROYS ACTION OR MOTION ABOVE OR BELOW ITS TOLERANCE BAND.

AXIOM 28:

THE MIND IS CONCERNED WHOLLY WITH THE ESTIMATION OF EFFORT.

DEFINITION: *Mind is the* theta *command post of any organism or organisms.*

AXIOM 29:

THE BASIC ERRORS OF REASON ARE FAILURE TO DIFFERENTIATE AMONGST MATTER, ENERGY, SPACE AND TIME.

AXIOM 30:

RIGHTNESS IS PROPER CALCULATION OF EFFORT.

AXIOM 31:

WRONGNESS IS ALWAYS MISCALCULATION OF EFFORT.

AXIOM 32:

THETA CAN EXERT ITSELF DIRECTLY OR EXTENSIONALLY.

Theta can direct physical application of the organism to the environment or, through the mind, can first calculate the action or extend, as in language, ideas.

Axiom 33:

Conclusions are directed toward the inhibition, maintenance or accelerations of efforts.

Axiom 34:

The common denominator of all life organisms is motion.

Axiom 35:

Effort of an organism to survive or succumb is physical motion of a life organism at a given moment in time through space.

Definition: *Motion is any change in orientation in space.*

Definition: *Force is random effort.*

Definition: *Effort is directed force.*

Axiom 36:

An organism's effort can be to remain at rest or persist in a given motion.

Static state has position in time, but an organism which is remaining positionally in a static state, if alive, is still continuing a highly complex pattern of motion, such as the heartbeat, digestion, etc.

The efforts of organisms to survive or succumb are assisted, compelled or opposed by the efforts of other organisms, matter, energy, space and time.

Definition: *Attention is a motion which must remain at an optimum effort.*

Attention is aberrated by becoming unfixed and sweeping at random or becoming too fixed without sweeping.

Unknown threats to survival when sensed cause attention to sweep without fixing.

Known threats to survival when sensed cause attention to fix.

AXIOM 37:

THE ULTIMATE GOAL OF *LAMBDA* IS INFINITE SURVIVAL.

AXIOM 38:

DEATH IS ABANDONMENT BY *THETA* OF A LIFE ORGANISM OR RACE OR SPECIES WHERE THESE CAN NO LONGER SERVE *THETA* IN ITS GOALS OF INFINITE SURVIVAL.

AXIOM 39:

THE REWARD OF AN ORGANISM ENGAGING UPON SURVIVAL ACTIVITY IS PLEASURE.

AXIOM 40:

THE PENALTY OF AN ORGANISM FAILING TO ENGAGE UPON SURVIVAL ACTIVITY, OR ENGAGING IN NON-SURVIVAL ACTIVITY, IS PAIN.

AXIOM 41:

THE CELL AND/OR VIRUS ARE THE PRIMARY BUILDING BLOCKS OF LIFE ORGANISMS.

AXIOM 42:

THE VIRUS AND CELL ARE MATTER AND ENERGY ANIMATED AND MOTIVATED IN SPACE AND TIME BY *THETA*.

AXIOM 43:

THETA MOBILIZES THE VIRUS AND CELL IN COLONIAL AGGREGATIONS TO INCREASE POTENTIAL MOTION AND ACCOMPLISH EFFORT.

AXIOM 44:

THE GOAL OF VIRUSES AND CELLS IS SURVIVAL IN SPACE THROUGH TIME.

AXIOM 45:

THE TOTAL MISSION OF HIGHER ORGANISMS, VIRUSES AND CELLS IS THE SAME AS THAT OF THE VIRUS AND CELL.

Axiom 46:

Colonial aggregations of viruses and cells can be imbued with more *theta* than they inherently contained.

Life energy joins any group whether a group of organisms or group of cells composing an organism. Here we have personal entity, individuation, etc.

Axiom 47:

Effort can be accomplished by *lambda* only through the coordination of its parts toward goals.

Axiom 48:

An organism is equipped to be governed and controlled by a mind.

Axiom 49:

The purpose of the mind is to pose and resolve problems relating to survival and to direct the effort of the organism according to these solutions.

Axiom 50:

All problems are posed and resolved through estimations of effort.

Axiom 51:

The mind can confuse position in space with position in time. (Counter-efforts producing action phrases.)

Axiom 52:

An organism proceeding toward survival is directed by the mind of that organism in the accomplishment of survival effort.

AXIOM 53:

AN ORGANISM PROCEEDING TOWARD SUCCUMB IS DIRECTED BY THE MIND OF THAT ORGANISM IN THE ACCOMPLISHMENT OF DEATH.

AXIOM 54:

SURVIVAL OF AN ORGANISM IS ACCOMPLISHED BY THE OVERCOMING OF EFFORTS OPPOSING ITS SURVIVAL. (Note: Corollary for other dynamics.)

DEFINITION: *Dynamic is the ability to translate solutions into action.*

AXIOM 55:

SURVIVAL EFFORT FOR AN ORGANISM INCLUDES THE DYNAMIC THRUST BY THAT ORGANISM FOR THE SURVIVAL OF ITSELF, ITS PROCREATION, ITS GROUP, ITS SUBSPECIES, ITS SPECIES, ALL LIFE ORGANISMS, MATERIAL UNIVERSE, THE LIFE STATIC AND, POSSIBLY, A SUPREME BEING. (Note: List of dynamics.)

AXIOM 56:

THE CYCLE OF AN ORGANISM, A GROUP OF ORGANISMS OR A SPECIES IS INCEPTION, GROWTH, RE-CREATION, DECAY AND DEATH.

AXIOM 57:

THE EFFORT OF AN ORGANISM IS DIRECTED TOWARD THE CONTROL OF THE ENVIRONMENT FOR ALL THE DYNAMICS.

AXIOM 58:

CONTROL OF AN ENVIRONMENT IS ACCOMPLISHED BY THE SUPPORT OF PRO-SURVIVAL FACTORS ALONG ANY DYNAMIC.

AXIOM 59:

ANY TYPE OF HIGHER ORGANISM IS ACCOMPLISHED BY THE EVOLUTION OF VIRUSES AND CELLS INTO FORMS CAPABLE OF BETTER EFFORTS TO CONTROL OR LIVE IN AN ENVIRONMENT.

Axiom 60:

The usefulness of an organism is determined by its ability to control the environment or to support organisms which control the environment.

Axiom 61:

An organism is rejected by *theta* to the degree that it fails in its goals.

Axiom 62:

Higher organisms can exist only in the degree that they are supported by the lower organisms.

Axiom 63:

The usefulness of an organism is determined by the alignment of its efforts toward survival.

Axiom 64:

The mind perceives and stores all data of the environment and aligns or fails to align these according to the time they were perceived.

DEFINITION: *A conclusion is the* theta facsimiles *of a group of combined data.*

DEFINITION: *A datum is a* theta facsimile *of physical action.*

Axiom 65:

The process of thought is the perception of the present and the comparison of it to the perceptions and conclusions of the past in order to direct action in the immediate or distant future.

COROLLARY: The attempt of thought is to perceive realities of the past and present in order to predict or postulate realities of the future.

AXIOM 66:

THE PROCESS BY WHICH LIFE EFFECTS ITS CONQUEST OF THE MATERIAL UNIVERSE CONSISTS IN THE CONVERSION OF THE POTENTIAL EFFORT OF MATTER AND ENERGY IN SPACE AND THROUGH TIME TO EFFECT WITH IT THE CONVERSION OF FURTHER MATTER AND ENERGY IN SPACE AND THROUGH TIME.

AXIOM 67:

THETA CONTAINS ITS OWN *THETA UNIVERSE* EFFORT WHICH TRANSLATES INTO *MEST* EFFORT.

AXIOM 68:

THE SINGLE ARBITRARY IN ANY ORGANISM IS TIME.

AXIOM 69:

PHYSICAL UNIVERSE PERCEPTIONS AND EFFORTS ARE RECEIVED BY AN ORGANISM AS FORCE WAVES, CONVERT BY FACSIMILE INTO *THETA* AND ARE THUS STORED.

DEFINITION: *Randomity is the misalignment through the internal or external efforts by other forms of life or the material universe of the efforts of an organism, and is imposed on the physical organism by counter-efforts in the environment.*

AXIOM 70:

ANY CYCLE OF ANY LIFE ORGANISM IS FROM STATIC TO MOTION TO STATIC.

AXIOM 71:

THE CYCLE OF RANDOMITY IS FROM STATIC, THROUGH OPTIMUM, THROUGH RANDOMITY SUFFICIENTLY REPETITIOUS OR SIMILAR TO CONSTITUTE ANOTHER STATIC.

AXIOM 72:

THERE ARE TWO SUBDIVISIONS TO RANDOMITY: DATA RANDOMITY AND FORCE RANDOMITY.

Axiom 73:

The three degrees of randomity consist of minus randomity, optimum randomity and plus randomity.

Definition: *Randomity is a component factor and necessary part of motion, if motion is to continue.*

Axiom 74:

Optimum randomity is necessary to learning.

Axiom 75:

The important factors in any area of randomity are effort and counter-effort. (Note: As distinguished from near-perceptions of effort.)

Axiom 76:

Randomity amongst organisms is vital to continuous survival of all organisms.

Axiom 77:

Theta affects the organism, other organisms and the physical universe by translating *theta facsimiles* into physical efforts or randomity of efforts.

Definition: *The degree of randomity is measured by the randomness of effort vectors within the organism, amongst organisms, amongst races or species of organisms or between organisms and the physical universe.*

Axiom 78:

Randomity becomes intense in indirect ratio to the time in which it takes place, modified by the total effort in the area.

Axiom 79:

Initial randomity can be reinforced by randomities of greater or lesser magnitude.

AXIOM 80:

AREAS OF RANDOMITY EXIST IN CHAINS OF SIMILARITY PLOTTED AGAINST TIME. THIS CAN BE TRUE OF WORDS AND ACTIONS CONTAINED IN RANDOMITIES. EACH MAY HAVE ITS OWN CHAIN PLOTTED AGAINST TIME.

AXIOM 81:

SANITY CONSISTS OF OPTIMUM RANDOMITY.

AXIOM 82:

ABERRATION EXISTS TO THE DEGREE THAT PLUS OR MINUS RANDOMITY EXISTS IN THE ENVIRONMENT OR PAST DATA OF AN ORGANISM, GROUP OR SPECIES MODIFIED BY THE ENDOWED SELF-DETERMINISM OF THAT ORGANISM, GROUP OR SPECIES.

AXIOM 83:

THE SELF-DETERMINISM OF AN ORGANISM IS DETERMINED BY ITS *THETA* ENDOWMENT, MODIFIED BY MINUS OR PLUS RANDOMITY IN ITS ENVIRONMENT OR ITS EXISTENCE.

AXIOM 84:

THE SELF-DETERMINISM OF AN ORGANISM IS INCREASED BY OPTIMUM RANDOMITY OF COUNTER-EFFORTS.

AXIOM 85:

THE SELF-DETERMINISM OF AN ORGANISM IS REDUCED BY PLUS OR MINUS RANDOMITY OF COUNTER-EFFORTS IN THE ENVIRONMENT.

AXIOM 86:

RANDOMITY CONTAINS BOTH THE RANDOMNESS OF EFFORTS AND THE VOLUME OF EFFORTS. (Note: An area of randomity can have a great deal of confusion but, without volume of energy, the confusion itself is negligible.)

Axiom 87:

That counter-effort is most acceptable to an organism which most closely appears to assist its accomplishment of its goal.

Axiom 88:

An area of severe plus or minus randomity can occlude data on any of the subjects of that plus or minus randomity which took place in a prior time. (Note: Shut-off mechanisms of earlier lives, perceptics, specific incidents, etc.)

Axiom 89:

Restimulation of plus, minus or optimum randomity can produce increased plus, minus or optimum randomity respectively in the organism.

Axiom 90:

An area of randomity can assume sufficient magnitude so as to appear to the organism as pain, according to its goals.

Axiom 91:

Past randomity can impose itself upon the present organism as *theta facsimiles*.

Axiom 92:

The engram is a severe area of plus or minus randomity of sufficient volume to cause unconsciousness.

Axiom 93:

Unconsciousness is an excess of randomity imposed by a counter-effort of sufficient force to cloud the awareness and direct function of the organism through the mind's control center.

AXIOM 94:

ANY COUNTER-EFFORT WHICH MISALIGNS THE ORGANISM'S COMMAND OF ITSELF OR ITS ENVIRONMENT ESTABLISHES PLUS OR MINUS RANDOMITY OR, IF OF SUFFICIENT MAGNITUDE, IS AN ENGRAM.

AXIOM 95:

PAST ENGRAMS ARE RESTIMULATED BY THE CONTROL CENTER'S PERCEPTION OF CIRCUMSTANCES SIMILAR TO THAT ENGRAM IN THE PRESENT ENVIRONMENT.

AXIOM 96:

AN ENGRAM IS A *THETA FACSIMILE* OF ATOMS AND MOLECULES IN MISALIGNMENT.

AXIOM 97:

ENGRAMS FIX EMOTIONAL RESPONSE AS THAT EMOTIONAL RESPONSE OF THE ORGANISM DURING THE RECEIPT OF THE COUNTER-EFFORT.

AXIOM 98:

FREE EMOTIONAL RESPONSE DEPENDS ON OPTIMUM RANDOMITY. IT DEPENDS UPON ABSENCE OF OR NON-RESTIMULATION OF ENGRAMS.

AXIOM 99:

THETA FACSIMILES CAN RECOMBINE INTO NEW SYMBOLS.

AXIOM 100:

LANGUAGE IS THE SYMBOLIZATION OF EFFORT.

AXIOM 101:

LANGUAGE DEPENDS FOR ITS FORCE UPON THE FORCE WHICH ACCOMPANIED ITS DEFINITION. (Note: Counter-effort, not language, is aberrative.)

AXIOM 102:

THE ENVIRONMENT CAN OCCLUDE THE CENTRAL CONTROL OF ANY ORGANISM AND ASSUME CONTROL OF THE MOTOR CONTROLS OF THAT ORGANISM. (Engram, restimulation, locks, hypnotism.)

AXIOM 103:

INTELLIGENCE DEPENDS ON THE ABILITY TO SELECT ALIGNED OR MISALIGNED DATA FROM AN AREA OF RANDOMITY AND SO DISCOVER A SOLUTION TO REDUCE ALL RANDOMITY IN THAT AREA.

AXIOM 104:

PERSISTENCE OBTAINS IN THE ABILITY OF THE MIND TO PUT SOLUTIONS INTO PHYSICAL ACTION TOWARD THE REALIZATION OF GOALS.

AXIOM 105:

AN UNKNOWN DATUM CAN PRODUCE DATA OF PLUS OR MINUS RANDOMITY.

AXIOM 106:

THE INTRODUCTION OF AN ARBITRARY FACTOR OR FORCE WITHOUT RECOURSE TO NATURAL LAWS OF THE BODY OR THE AREA INTO WHICH THE ARBITRARY IS INTRODUCED BRINGS ABOUT PLUS OR MINUS RANDOMITY.

AXIOM 107:

DATA OF PLUS OR MINUS RANDOMITY DEPENDS FOR ITS CONFUSION ON FORMER PLUS OR MINUS RANDOMITY OR ABSENT DATA.

AXIOM 108:

EFFORTS WHICH ARE INHIBITED OR COMPELLED BY EXTERIOR EFFORTS EFFECT A PLUS OR MINUS RANDOMITY OF EFFORTS.

AXIOM 109:

BEHAVIOR IS MODIFIED BY COUNTER-EFFORTS WHICH HAVE IMPINGED ON THE ORGANISM.

AXIOM 110:

THE COMPONENT PARTS OF *THETA* ARE AFFINITY, REALITY AND COMMUNICATION.

AXIOM 111:

SELF-DETERMINISM CONSISTS OF MAXIMAL AFFINITY, REALITY AND COMMUNICATION.

AXIOM 112:

AFFINITY IS THE COHESION OF *THETA*.

Affinity manifests itself as the recognition of similarity of efforts and goals amongst organisms by those organisms.

AXIOM 113:

REALITY IS THE AGREEMENT UPON PERCEPTIONS AND DATA IN THE PHYSICAL UNIVERSE.

All that we can be sure is real is that on which we have agreed is real. Agreement is the essence of reality.

AXIOM 114:

COMMUNICATION IS THE INTERCHANGE OF PERCEPTION THROUGH THE MATERIAL UNIVERSE BETWEEN ORGANISMS OR THE PERCEPTION OF THE MATERIAL UNIVERSE BY SENSE CHANNELS.

AXIOM 115:

SELF-DETERMINISM IS THE *THETA* CONTROL OF THE ORGANISM.

Axiom 116:

A self-determined effort is that counter-effort which has been received into the organism in the past and integrated into the organism for its conscious use.

Axiom 117:

The components of self-determinism are Affinity, Communication and Reality.

Self-determinism is manifested along each dynamic.

Axiom 118:

An organism cannot become aberrated unless it has agreed upon that aberration, has been in communication with a source of aberration and has had affinity for the aberrator.

Axiom 119:

Agreement with any source contra- or pro-survival postulates a new reality for the organism.

Axiom 120:

Non-survival courses, thoughts and actions require non-optimum effort.

Axiom 121:

Every thought has been preceded by physical action.

Axiom 122:

The mind does with thought as it has done with entities in the physical universe.

Axiom 123:

All effort concerned with pain is concerned with loss.

Organisms hold pain and engrams to them as a latent effort to prevent loss of some portion of the organism. All loss is a loss of motion.

AXIOM 124:

THE AMOUNT OF COUNTER-EFFORT THE ORGANISM CAN OVERCOME IS PROPORTIONAL TO THE *THETA* ENDOWMENT OF THE ORGANISM, MODIFIED BY THE PHYSIQUE OF THAT ORGANISM.

AXIOM 125:

EXCESSIVE COUNTER-EFFORT TO THE EFFORT OF A LIFE ORGANISM PRODUCES UNCONSCIOUSNESS.

COROLLARY: UNCONSCIOUSNESS GIVES THE SUPPRESSION OF AN ORGANISM'S CONTROL CENTER BY COUNTER-EFFORT.

DEFINITION: *The control center of the organism can be defined as the contact point between* theta *and the physical universe and is that center which is aware of being aware and which has charge of and responsibility for the organism along all its dynamics.*

AXIOM 126:

PERCEPTIONS ARE ALWAYS RECEIVED IN THE CONTROL CENTER OF AN ORGANISM WHETHER THE CONTROL CENTER IS IN CONTROL OF THE ORGANISM AT THE TIME OR NOT.

This is an explanation for the assumption of valences.

AXIOM 127:

ALL PERCEPTIONS REACHING THE ORGANISM'S SENSE CHANNELS ARE RECORDED AND STORED BY *THETA FACSIMILE*.

DEFINITION: *Perception is the process of recording data from the physical universe and storing it as a* theta facsimile.

DEFINITION: *Recall is the process of regaining perceptions.*

Axiom 128:

ANY ORGANISM CAN RECALL EVERYTHING WHICH IT HAS PERCEIVED.

Axiom 129:

AN ORGANISM DISPLACED BY PLUS OR MINUS RANDOMITY IS THEREAFTER REMOTE FROM THE PERCEPTION RECORDING CENTER.

Increased remoteness brings about occlusions of perceptions. One can perceive things in present time and then, because they are being recorded after they passed *theta* perception of the awareness unit, they are recorded but cannot be recalled.

Axiom 130:

THETA FACSIMILES OF COUNTER-EFFORT ARE ALL THAT INTERPOSE BETWEEN THE CONTROL CENTER AND ITS RECALLS.

Axiom 131:

ANY COUNTER-EFFORT RECEIVED INTO A CONTROL CENTER IS ALWAYS ACCOMPANIED BY ALL PERCEPTICS.

Axiom 132:

THE RANDOM COUNTER-EFFORTS TO AN ORGANISM AND THE INTERMINGLED PERCEPTIONS IN THE RANDOMITY CAN RE-EXERT THAT FORCE UPON AN ORGANISM WHEN RESTIMULATED.

DEFINITION: *Restimulation is the reactivation of a past counter-effort by appearance in the organism's environment of a similarity toward the content of the past randomity area.*

Axiom 133:

SELF-DETERMINISM ALONE BRINGS ABOUT THE MECHANISM OF RESTIMULATION.

AXIOM 134:

A REACTIVATED AREA OF THE PAST RANDOMITY IMPINGES THE EFFORT AND THE PERCEPTIONS UPON THE ORGANISM.

AXIOM 135:

ACTIVATION OF A RANDOMITY AREA IS ACCOMPLISHED FIRST BY THE PERCEPTIONS, THEN BY THE PAIN, FINALLY BY THE EFFORT.

AXIOM 136:

THE MIND IS PLASTICALLY CAPABLE OF RECORDING ALL EFFORTS AND COUNTER-EFFORTS.

AXIOM 137:

A COUNTER-EFFORT ACCOMPANIED BY SUFFICIENT (ENRANDOMED) FORCE IMPRESSES THE FACSIMILE OF THE COUNTER-EFFORT PERSONALITY INTO THE MIND OF AN ORGANISM.

AXIOM 138:

ABERRATION IS THE DEGREE OF RESIDUAL PLUS OR MINUS RANDOMITY ACCUMULATED BY COMPELLING, INHIBITING, OR UNWARRANTED ASSISTING OF EFFORTS ON THE PART OF OTHER ORGANISMS OR THE PHYSICAL (MATERIAL) UNIVERSE.

Aberration is caused by what is done to the individual, not what the individual does, plus his self-determinism about what has been done to him.

AXIOM 139:

ABERRATED BEHAVIOR CONSISTS OF DESTRUCTIVE EFFORT TOWARD PRO-SURVIVAL DATA OR ENTITIES ON ANY DYNAMIC, OR EFFORT TOWARD THE SURVIVAL OF CONTRA-SURVIVAL DATA OR ENTITIES FOR ANY DYNAMIC.

AXIOM 140:

A VALENCE IS A FACSIMILE PERSONALITY MADE CAPABLE OF FORCE BY THE COUNTER-EFFORT OF THE MOMENT OF RECEIPT INTO THE PLUS OR MINUS RANDOMITY OF UNCONSCIOUSNESS.

Valences are assistive, compulsive or inhibitive to the organism.

A CONTROL CENTER IS NOT A VALENCE.

AXIOM 141:

A CONTROL CENTER EFFORT IS ALIGNED TOWARD A GOAL THROUGH DEFINITE SPACE AS A RECOGNIZED INCIDENT IN TIME.

AXIOM 142:

AN ORGANISM IS AS HEALTHY AND SANE AS IT IS SELF-DETERMINED.

The environmental control of the organism motor controls inhibits the organism's ability to change with the changing environment, since the organism will attempt to carry forward with one set of responses when it needs by self-determinism to create another to survive in another environment.

AXIOM 143:

ALL LEARNING IS ACCOMPLISHED BY RANDOM EFFORT.

AXIOM 144:

A COUNTER-EFFORT PRODUCING SUFFICIENT PLUS OR MINUS RANDOMITY TO RECORD IS RECORDED WITH AN INDEX OF SPACE AND TIME AS HIDDEN AS THE REMAINDER OF ITS CONTENT.

AXIOM 145:

A COUNTER-EFFORT PRODUCING SUFFICIENT PLUS OR MINUS RANDOMITY WHEN ACTIVATED BY RESTIMULATION EXERTS ITSELF AGAINST THE ENVIRONMENT OR THE ORGANISM WITHOUT REGARD TO SPACE AND TIME, EXCEPT REACTIVATED PERCEPTIONS.

AXIOM 146:

COUNTER-EFFORTS ARE DIRECTED OUT FROM THE ORGANISM UNTIL THEY ARE FURTHER ENRANDOMED BY THE ENVIRON AT WHICH TIME THEY AGAIN ACTIVATE AGAINST THE CONTROL CENTER.

AXIOM 147:

AN ORGANISM'S MIND EMPLOYS COUNTER-EFFORTS EFFECTIVELY ONLY SO LONG AS INSUFFICIENT PLUS OR MINUS RANDOMITY EXISTS TO HIDE DIFFERENTIATION OF THE FACSIMILES CREATED.

AXIOM 148:

PHYSICAL LAWS ARE LEARNED BY LIFE ENERGY ONLY BY IMPINGEMENT OF THE PHYSICAL UNIVERSE PRODUCING RANDOMITY, AND A WITHDRAWAL FROM THAT IMPINGEMENT.

AXIOM 149:

LIFE DEPENDS UPON AN ALIGNMENT OF FORCE VECTORS IN THE DIRECTION OF SURVIVAL AND THE NULLIFICATION OF FORCE VECTORS IN THE DIRECTION OF SUCCUMB IN ORDER TO SURVIVE.

> COROLLARY: LIFE DEPENDS UPON AN ALIGNMENT OF FORCE VECTORS IN THE DIRECTION OF SUCCUMB AND THE NULLIFICATION OF FORCE VECTORS IN THE DIRECTION OF SURVIVE IN ORDER TO SUCCUMB.

AXIOM 150:

ANY AREA OF RANDOMITY GATHERS TO IT SITUATIONS SIMILAR TO IT WHICH DO NOT CONTAIN ACTUAL EFFORTS BUT ONLY PERCEPTIONS.

Axiom 151:

Whether an organism has the goal of surviving or succumbing depends upon the amount of plus or minus randomity it has reactivated. (Not residual.)

Axiom 152:

Survival is accomplished only by motion.

Axiom 153:

In the physical universe the absence of motion is vanishment.

Axiom 154:

Death is the equivalent to life of total lack of life-motivated motion.

Axiom 155:

Acquisition of pro-survival matter and energy or organisms in space and time means increased motion.

Axiom 156:

Loss of pro-survival matter and energy or organisms in space and time means decreased motion.

Axiom 157:

Acquisition or proximity of matter, energy or organisms which assist the survival of an organism increase the survival potentials of an organism.

Axiom 158:

Acquisition or proximity of matter, energy or organisms which inhibit the survival of an organism decrease its survival potential.

AXIOM 159:

GAIN OF SURVIVAL ENERGY, MATTER OR ORGANISMS INCREASES THE FREEDOM OF AN ORGANISM.

AXIOM 160:

RECEIPT OR PROXIMITY OF NON-SURVIVAL ENERGY, MATTER OR TIME DECREASES THE FREEDOM OF MOTION OF AN ORGANISM.

AXIOM 161:

THE CONTROL CENTER ATTEMPTS THE HALTING OR LENGTHENING OF TIME, THE EXPANSION OR CONTRACTION OF SPACE AND THE DECREASE OR INCREASE OF ENERGY AND MATTER.

This is a primary source of invalidation, and it is also a primary source of aberration.

AXIOM 162:

PAIN IS THE BALK OF EFFORT BY COUNTER-EFFORT IN GREAT INTENSITY, WHETHER THAT EFFORT IS TO REMAIN AT REST OR IN MOTION.

AXIOM 163:

PERCEPTION, INCLUDING PAIN, CAN BE EXHAUSTED FROM AN AREA OF PLUS OR MINUS RANDOMITY STILL LEAVING THE EFFORT AND COUNTER-EFFORT OF THAT PLUS OR MINUS RANDOMITY.

AXIOM 164:

THE RATIONALITY OF THE MIND DEPENDS UPON AN OPTIMUM REACTION TOWARD TIME.

DEFINITION: *Sanity, the computation of futures.*

DEFINITION: *Neurotic, the computation of present time only.*

DEFINITION: *Psychotic, computation only of past situations.*

AXIOM 165:

SURVIVAL PERTAINS ONLY TO THE FUTURE.

> COROLLARY: SUCCUMB PERTAINS ONLY TO THE PRESENT AND PAST.

AXIOM 166:

AN INDIVIDUAL IS AS HAPPY AS HE CAN PERCEIVE SURVIVAL POTENTIALS IN THE FUTURE.

AXIOM 167:

AS THE NEEDS OF ANY ORGANISM ARE MET IT RISES HIGHER AND HIGHER IN ITS EFFORTS ALONG THE DYNAMICS.

An organism which achieves ARC with itself can better achieve ARC with sex in the future; having achieved this it can achieve ARC with groups; having achieved this, it can achieve ARC with Mankind, etc.

AXIOM 168:

AFFINITY, REALITY AND COMMUNICATION CO-EXIST IN AN INEXTRICABLE RELATIONSHIP.

The co-existent relationship between Affinity, Reality and Communication is such that none can be increased without increasing the other two and none can be decreased without decreasing the other two.

AXIOM 169:

ANY AESTHETIC PRODUCT IS A SYMBOLIC FACSIMILE OR COMBINATION OF FACSIMILES OF *THETA* OR PHYSICAL UNIVERSES IN VARIED RANDOMITIES AND VOLUMES OF RANDOMITIES WITH THE INTERPLAY OF TONES.

AXIOM 170:

AN AESTHETIC PRODUCT IS AN INTERPRETATION OF THE UNIVERSES BY AN INDIVIDUAL OR GROUP MIND.

AXIOM 171:

DELUSION IS THE POSTULATION BY THE IMAGINATION OF OCCURRENCES IN AREAS OF PLUS OR MINUS RANDOMITY.

AXIOM 172:

DREAMS ARE THE IMAGINATIVE RECONSTRUCTION OF AREAS OF RANDOMITY OR THE RE-SYMBOLIZATION OF THE EFFORTS OF *THETA*.

AXIOM 173:

A MOTION IS CREATED BY THE DEGREE OF OPTIMUM RANDOMITY INTRODUCED BY THE COUNTER-EFFORT TO AN ORGANISM'S EFFORT.

AXIOM 174:

MEST, WHICH HAS BEEN MOBILIZED BY LIFE FORMS, IS IN MORE AFFINITY WITH LIFE ORGANISMS THAN NON-MOBILIZED *MEST*.

AXIOM 175:

ALL PAST PERCEPTION, CONCLUSION AND EXISTENCE MOMENTS, INCLUDING THOSE OF PLUS OR MINUS RANDOMITY, ARE RECOVERABLE TO THE CONTROL CENTER OF THE ORGANISM.

AXIOM 176:

THE ABILITY TO PRODUCE SURVIVAL EFFORT ON THE PART OF AN ORGANISM IS AFFECTED BY THE DEGREES OF RANDOMITY EXISTING IN ITS PAST. (This includes learning.)

AXIOM 177:

AREAS OF PAST PLUS OR MINUS RANDOMITY CAN BE READDRESSED BY THE CONTROL CENTER OF AN ORGANISM AND THE PLUS OR MINUS RANDOMITY EXHAUSTED.

AXIOM 178:

THE EXHAUSTION OF PAST PLUS OR MINUS RANDOMITIES
PERMITS THE CONTROL CENTER OF AN ORGANISM TO EFFECT
ITS OWN EFFORTS TOWARD SURVIVAL GOALS.

AXIOM 179:

THE EXHAUSTION OF SELF-DETERMINED EFFORT FROM A
PAST AREA OF PLUS OR MINUS RANDOMITY NULLIFIES THE
EFFECTIVENESS OF THAT AREA.

AXIOM 180:

PAIN IS THE RANDOMITY PRODUCED BY SUDDEN OR STRONG
COUNTER-EFFORTS.

AXIOM 181:

PAIN IS STORED AS PLUS OR MINUS RANDOMITY.

AXIOM 182:

PAIN, AS AN AREA OF PLUS OR MINUS RANDOMITY, CAN
REINFLICT ITSELF UPON THE ORGANISM.

AXIOM 183:

PAST PAIN BECOMES INEFFECTIVE UPON THE ORGANISM WHEN
THE RANDOMITY OF ITS AREA IS ADDRESSED AND ALIGNED.

AXIOM 184:

THE EARLIER THE AREA OF PLUS OR MINUS RANDOMITY, THE
GREATER SELF-PRODUCED EFFORT EXISTED TO REPEL IT.

AXIOM 185:

LATER AREAS OF PLUS OR MINUS RANDOMITY CANNOT BE
REALIGNED EASILY UNTIL EARLIER AREAS ARE REALIGNED.

AXIOM 186:

AREAS OF PLUS OR MINUS RANDOMITY BECOME INCREASED IN
ACTIVITY WHEN PERCEPTIONS OF SIMILARITY ARE INTRODUCED
INTO THEM.

AXIOM 187:

PAST AREAS OF PLUS OR MINUS RANDOMITY CAN BE REDUCED AND ALIGNED BY ADDRESS TO THEM IN PRESENT TIME.

AXIOM 188:

ABSOLUTE GOOD AND ABSOLUTE EVIL DO NOT EXIST IN THE *MEST* UNIVERSE.

AXIOM 189:

THAT WHICH IS GOOD FOR AN ORGANISM MAY BE DEFINED AS THAT WHICH PROMOTES THE SURVIVAL OF THAT ORGANISM.

COROLLARY: EVIL MAY BE DEFINED AS THAT WHICH INHIBITS OR BRINGS PLUS OR MINUS RANDOMITY INTO THE ORGANISM, WHICH IS CONTRARY TO THE SURVIVAL MOTIVES OF THE ORGANISM.

AXIOM 190:

HAPPINESS CONSISTS IN THE ACT OF BRINGING ALIGNMENT INTO HITHERTO RESISTING PLUS OR MINUS RANDOMITY. NEITHER THE ACT OR ACTION OF ATTAINING SURVIVAL, NOR THE ACCOMPLISHMENT OF THIS ACT ITSELF, BRINGS ABOUT HAPPINESS.

AXIOM 191:

CONSTRUCTION IS AN ALIGNMENT OF DATA.

COROLLARY: DESTRUCTION IS A PLUS OR MINUS RANDOMITY OF DATA.

The effort of construction is the alignment toward the survival of the aligning organism.

Destruction is the effort of bringing randomity into an area.

AXIOM 192:

OPTIMUM SURVIVAL BEHAVIOR CONSISTS OF EFFORT IN THE MAXIMUM SURVIVAL INTEREST IN EVERYTHING CONCERNED IN THE DYNAMICS.

Axiom 193:

The optimum survival solution of any problem would consist of the highest attainable survival for every dynamic concerned.

Axiom 194:

The worth of any organism consists of its value to the survival of its own *theta* along any dynamic.

APPENDIX

*F*URTHER STUDY
Books & Lectures by L. Ron Hubbard

The materials of Dianetics and Scientology comprise the largest body of information ever assembled on the mind, spirit and life, rigorously refined and codified by L. Ron Hubbard through five decades of research, investigation and development. The results of that work are contained in hundreds of books and more than 3,000 recorded lectures. A full listing and description of them all can be obtained from any Scientology Church or Publications Organization. (See *Guide to the Materials*.)

The books and lectures below form the foundation upon which the Bridge to Freedom is built. They are listed in the sequence Ron wrote or delivered them. In many instances, Ron gave a series of lectures immediately following the release of a new book to provide further explanation and insight of these milestones. Through monumental restoration efforts, those lectures are now available and are listed herein with their companion book.

While Ron's books contain the summaries of breakthroughs and conclusions as they appeared in the developmental research track, his lectures provide the running day-to-day record of research and explain the thoughts, conclusions, tests and demonstrations that lay along that route. In that regard, they are the complete record of the entire research track, providing not only the most important breakthroughs in Man's history, but the *why* and *how* Ron arrived at them.

Not the least advantage of a chronological study of these books and lectures is the inclusion of words and terms which, when originally used, were defined by LRH with considerable exactitude. Far beyond a mere "definition," entire lectures are devoted to a full description of each new Dianetic or Scientology term—what made the breakthrough possible, its application in auditing as well as its application to life itself. As a result, one leaves behind no misunderstoods, obtains a full conceptual understanding of Dianetics and Scientology and grasps the subjects at a level not otherwise possible.

Through a sequential study, you can see how the subject progressed and recognize the highest levels of development. The listing of books and lectures below shows where *Advanced Procedure and Axioms* fits within the developmental line. From there you can determine your *next* step or any earlier books and lectures you may have missed. You will then be able to fill in missing gaps, not only gaining knowledge of each breakthrough, but greater understanding of what you've already studied.

This is the path to knowing how to know, unlocking the gates to your future eternity. Follow it.

DIANETICS: THE ORIGINAL THESIS • Ron's *first* description of Dianetics. Originally circulated in manuscript form, it was soon copied and passed from hand to hand. Ensuing word of mouth created such demand for more information, Ron concluded the only way to answer the inquiries was with a book. That book was Dianetics: The Modern Science of Mental Health, now the all-time self-help bestseller. Find out what started it all. For here is the bedrock foundation of Dianetic discoveries: the *Original Axioms*, the *Dynamic Principle of Existence*, the *Anatomy of the Analytical* and *Reactive Mind*, the *Dynamics*, the *Tone Scale*, the *Auditor's Code* and the first description of a *Clear*. Even more than that, here are the primary laws describing *how* and *why* auditing works. It's only here in Dianetics: The Original Thesis.

DIANETICS: THE EVOLUTION OF A SCIENCE • This is the story of *how* Ron discovered the reactive mind and developed the procedures to get rid of it. Originally written for a national magazine—published to coincide with the release of Dianetics: The Modern Science of Mental Health—it started a wildfire movement virtually overnight upon that book's publication. Here then are both the fundamentals of Dianetics as well as the only account of Ron's two-decade journey of discovery and how he applied a scientific methodology to the problems of the human mind. He wrote it so you would know. Hence, this book is a must for every Dianeticist and Scientologist.

DIANETICS: THE MODERN SCIENCE OF MENTAL HEALTH • The bolt from the blue that began a worldwide movement. For while Ron had previously announced his discovery of the reactive mind, it had only fueled the fire of those wanting more information. More to the point—it was humanly impossible for one man to clear an entire planet. Encompassing all his previous discoveries and case histories of those breakthroughs in application, Ron provided the complete handbook of Dianetics procedure to train auditors to use it everywhere. A bestseller for more than half a century and with tens of millions of copies in print, Dianetics: The Modern Science of Mental Health has been translated in more than fifty languages, and used in more than 100 countries of Earth—indisputably, the most widely read and influential book about the human mind ever written. And that is why it will forever be known as *Book One*.

    DIANETICS LECTURES AND DEMONSTRATIONS • Immediately following the publication of *Dianetics*, LRH began lecturing to packed auditoriums across America. Although addressing thousands at a time, demand continued to grow. To meet that demand, his presentation in Oakland, California, was recorded. In these four lectures, Ron related the events that sparked his investigation and his personal journey to his groundbreaking discoveries. He followed it all with a personal demonstration of Dianetics auditing—the only such demonstration of Book One available. *4 lectures.*

FURTHER STUDY

DIANETICS PROFESSIONAL COURSE LECTURES—*A SPECIAL COURSE FOR BOOK ONE AUDITORS* • Following six months of coast-to-coast travel, lecturing to the first Dianeticists, Ron assembled auditors in Los Angeles for a new Professional Course. The subject was his next sweeping discovery on life—the *ARC Triangle*, describing the interrelationship of *Affinity, Reality* and *Communication*. Through a series of fifteen lectures, LRH announced many firsts, including the *Spectrum of Logic*, containing an infinity of gradients from right to wrong; *ARC and the Dynamics;* the *Tone Scales of ARC;* the *Auditor's Code* and how it relates to ARC; and the *Accessibility Chart* that classifies a case and how to process it. Here, then, is both the final statement on Book One Auditing Procedures and the discovery upon which all further research would advance. The data in these lectures was thought to be lost for over fifty years and only available in student notes published in Notes on the Lectures. The original recordings have now been discovered making them broadly available for the first time. Life in its highest state, *Understanding*, is composed of Affinity, Reality and Communication. And, as LRH said, the best description of the ARC Triangle to be found anywhere is in these lectures. *15 lectures.*

SCIENCE OF SURVIVAL—*PREDICTION OF HUMAN BEHAVIOR* • The most useful book you will ever own. Built around the *Hubbard Chart of Human Evaluation*, Science of Survival provides the first accurate prediction of human behavior. Included on the chart are all the manifestations of an individual's survival potential graduated from highest to lowest, making this the complete book on the Tone Scale. Knowing only one or two characteristics of a person and using this chart, you can plot his or her position on the Tone Scale and thereby know the rest, obtaining an accurate index of their *entire* personality, conduct and character. Before this book the world was convinced that cases could not improve but only deteriorate. Science of Survival presents the idea of different states of case and the brand-new idea that one can progress upward on the Tone Scale. And therein lies the basis of today's Grade Chart.

THE SCIENCE OF SURVIVAL LECTURES • Underlying the development of the Tone Scale and Chart of Human Evaluation was a monumental breakthrough: The *Theta–MEST Theory*, containing the explanation of the interaction between Life—*theta*—with the physical universe of Matter, Energy, Space and Time—*MEST*. In these lectures, delivered to students immediately following publication of the book, Ron gave the most expansive description of all that lies behind the Chart of Human Evaluation and its application in life itself. Moreover, here also is the explanation of how the ratio of *theta* and *en(turbulated)-theta* determines one's position on the Tone Scale and the means to ascend to higher states. *4 lectures.*

SELF ANALYSIS • The barriers of life are really just shadows. Learn to know yourself—not just a shadow of yourself. Containing the most complete description of consciousness, Self Analysis takes you through your past, through your potentials, your life. First, with a series of self-examinations and using a special version of the Hubbard Chart of Human Evaluation, you plot yourself on the Tone Scale. Then, applying a series of light yet powerful processes, you embark on the great adventure of self-discovery. This book further contains embracive principles that reach *any* case, from the lowest to the highest—including auditing techniques so effective they are referred to by Ron again and again through all following years of research into the highest states. In sum, this book not only moves one up the Tone Scale but can pull a person out of almost anything.

ADVANCED PROCEDURE AND AXIOMS • *(This current volume.)* With new breakthroughs on the nature and anatomy of engrams—"Engrams are effective only when the individual himself determines that they will be effective"—came the discovery of the being's use of a *Service Facsimile:* a mechanism employed to explain away failures in life, but which then locks a person into detrimental patterns of behavior and further failure. In consequence came a new type of processing addressing *Thought, Emotion* and *Effort* detailed in the "Fifteen Acts" of Advanced Procedure and oriented to the rehabilitation of the preclear's *Self-determinism.* Hence, this book also contains the all-encompassing, no-excuses-allowed explanation of *Full Responsibility,* the key to unlocking it all. Moreover, here is the codification of *Definitions, Logics,* and *Axioms,* providing both the summation of the entire subject and direction for all future research. *See Handbook for Preclears, written as a companion self-processing manual to Advanced Procedure and Axioms.*

> **THOUGHT, EMOTION AND EFFORT** • With the codification of the Axioms came the means to address key points on a case that could unravel all aberration. *Basic Postulates, Prime Thought, Cause and Effect* and their effect on everything from *memory* and *responsibility* to an individual's own role in empowering *engrams*—these matters are only addressed in this series. Here, too, is the most complete description of the *Service Facsimile* found anywhere—and why its resolution removes an individual's self-imposed disabilities. *21 lectures.*

HANDBOOK FOR PRECLEARS • The "Fifteen Acts" of Advanced Procedure and Axioms are paralleled by the fifteen Self-processing Acts given in Handbook for Preclears. Moreover, this book contains several essays giving the most expansive description of the *Ideal State of Man*. Discover why behavior patterns become so solidly fixed; why habits seemingly can't be broken; how decisions long ago have more power over a person than his decisions today; and why a person keeps past negative experiences in the present. It's all clearly laid out on the Chart of Attitudes—a milestone breakthrough that complements the Chart of Human Evaluation—plotting the ideal state of being and one's *attitudes* and *reactions* to life. *In self-processing, Handbook for Preclears is used in conjunction with Self Analysis.*

THE LIFE CONTINUUM • Besieged with requests for lectures on his latest breakthroughs, Ron replied with everything they wanted and more at the Second Annual Conference of Dianetic Auditors. Describing the technology that lies behind the self-processing steps of the *Handbook*—here is the *how* and *why* of it all: the discovery of *Life Continuum*—the mechanism by which an individual is compelled to carry on the life of another deceased or departed individual, generating in his own body the infirmities and mannerisms of the departed. Combined with auditor instruction on use of the Chart of Attitudes in determining how to enter every case at the proper gradient, here, too, are directions for dissemination of the Handbook and hence, the means to begin wide-scale clearing. *10 lectures.*

SCIENTOLOGY: MILESTONE ONE • Ron began the first lecture in this series with six words that would change the world forever: "This is a course in *Scientology*." From there, Ron not only described the vast scope of this, a then brand-new subject, he also detailed his discoveries on past lives. He proceeded from there to the description of the first E-Meter and its initial use in uncovering the *theta line* (the entire track of a thetan's existence), as entirely distinct from the *genetic body line* (the time track of bodies and their physical evolution), shattering the "one-life" lie and revealing the *whole track* of spiritual existence. Here, then, is the very genesis of Scientology. *22 lectures.*

THE ROUTE TO INFINITY: TECHNIQUE 80 LECTURES • As Ron explained, "Technique 80 is the *To Be or Not To Be* Technique." With that, he unveiled the crucial foundation on which ability and sanity rest: *the being's capacity to make a decision*. Here, then, is the anatomy of "maybe," the *Wavelengths of ARC*, the *Tone Scale of Decisions*, and the means to rehabilitate a being's ability *To Be* ... almost *anything*. *7 lectures. (Knowledge of Technique 80 is required for Technique 88 as described in Scientology: A History of Man—below.)*

SCIENTOLOGY: A HISTORY OF MAN • "A cold-blooded and factual account of your last 76 trillion years." So begins A History of Man, announcing the revolutionary *Technique 88*—revealing for the first time the truth about whole track experience and the exclusive address, in auditing, to the thetan. Here is history unraveled with the first E-Meter, delineating and describing the principal incidents on the whole track to be found in any human being: *Electronic implants, entities,* the *genetic track, between-lives incidents, how bodies evolved* and *why you got trapped in them*—they're all detailed here.

TECHNIQUE 88: INCIDENTS ON THE TRACK BEFORE EARTH • "Technique 88 is the most hyperbolical, effervescent, dramatic, unexaggeratable, high-flown, superlative, grandiose, colossal and magnificent technique which the mind of Man could conceivably embrace. It is as big as the whole track and all the incidents on it. It's what you apply it to; it's what's been going on. It contains the riddles and secrets, the mysteries of all time. You could bannerline this technique like they do a sideshow, but nothing you could say, no adjective you could use, would adequately describe even a small segment of it. It not only batters the imagination, it makes you ashamed to imagine anything," is Ron's introduction to you in this never-before-available lecture series, expanding on all else contained in History of Man. What awaits you is the whole track itself. *15 lectures.*

SCIENTOLOGY 8-80 • The *first* explanation of the electronics of human thought and the energy phenomena in any being. Discover how even physical universe laws of motion are mirrored in a being, not to mention the electronics of aberration. Here is the link between theta and MEST revealing what energy *is*, and how you *create* it. It was this breakthrough that revealed the subject of a thetan's *flows* and which, in turn, is applied in *every* auditing process today. In the book's title, "8-8" stands for *Infinity-Infinity*, and "0" represents the static, *theta*. Included are the *Wavelengths of Emotion, Aesthetics, Beauty and Ugliness, Inflow and Outflow* and the *Sub-zero Tone Scale*—applicable only to the thetan.

SOURCE OF LIFE ENERGY • Beginning with the announcement of his new book—Scientology 8-80—Ron not only unveiled his breakthroughs of theta as the Source of Life Energy, but detailed the *Methods of Research* he used to make that and every other discovery of Dianetics and Scientology: the *Qs* and *Logics*—methods of *thinking* applicable to any universe or thinking process. Here, then, is both *how to think* and *how to evaluate all data and knowledge,* and thus, the linchpin to a full understanding of both Scientology and life itself. *14 lectures.*

FURTHER STUDY

THE COMMAND OF THETA • While in preparation of his newest book and the Doctorate Course he was about to deliver, Ron called together auditors for a new Professional Course. As he said, "For the first time with this class we are stepping, really, beyond the scope of the word *Survival*." From that vantage point, the Command of Theta gives the technology that bridges the knowledge from 8-80 to 8-8008, and provides the first full explanation of the subject of *Cause* and a permanent shift of orientation in life from MEST to *Theta*. *10 lectures.*

SCIENTOLOGY 8-8008 • The complete description of the behavior and potentials of a *thetan*, and textbook for the Philadelphia Doctorate Course and The Factors: Admiration and the Renaissance of Beingness lectures. As Ron said, the book's title serves to fix in the mind of the individual a route by which he can rehabilitate himself, his abilities, his ethics and his goals—the attainment of *infinity* (8) by the reduction of the apparent *infinity* (8) of the MEST universe to *zero* (0) and the increase of the apparent *zero* (0) of one's own universe to *infinity* (8). Condensed herein are more than 80,000 hours of investigation, with a summarization and amplification of every breakthrough to date—and the full significance of those discoveries form the new vantage point of *Operating Thetan.*

THE PHILADELPHIA DOCTORATE COURSE LECTURES • This renowned series stands as the largest single body of work on the anatomy, behavior and potentials of the spirit of Man ever assembled, providing the very fundamentals which underlie the route to Operating Thetan. Here it is in complete detail—the thetan's relationship to the *creation, maintenance* and *destruction of universes.* In just those terms, here is the *anatomy* of matter, energy, space and time, and *postulating* universes into existence. Here, too, is the thetan's fall from whole track abilities and the *universal laws* by which they are restored. In short, here is Ron's codification of the upper echelon of theta beingness and behavior. Lecture after lecture fully expands every concept of the course text, Scientology 8-8008, providing the total scope of *you* in native state. *76 lectures and accompanying reproductions of the original 54 LRH hand-drawn lecture charts.*

THE FACTORS: ADMIRATION AND THE RENAISSANCE OF BEINGNESS • With the *potentials* of a thetan fully established came a look outward resulting in Ron's monumental discovery of a *universal solvent* and the basic laws of the theta *universe*—laws quite literally senior to anything: *The Factors: Summation of the Considerations of the Human Spirit and Material Universe.* So dramatic were these breakthroughs, Ron expanded the book Scientology 8-8008, both clarifying previous discoveries and adding chapter after chapter which, studied with these lectures, provide a postgraduate level to the Doctorate Course. Here then are lectures containing the knowledge of *universal truth* unlocking the riddle of creation itself. *18 lectures.*

207

ADVANCED PROCEDURE AND AXIOMS
L. RON HUBBARD

THE CREATION OF HUMAN ABILITY—*A HANDBOOK FOR SCIENTOLOGISTS* • On the heels of his discoveries of Operating Thetan came a year of intensive research, exploring the realm of a *thetan exterior.* Through auditing and instruction, including 450 lectures in this same twelve-month span, Ron codified the entire subject of Scientology. And it's all contained in this handbook, from a *Summary of Scientology* to its basic *Axioms* and *Codes.* Moreover, here is *Intensive Procedure,* containing the famed Exteriorization Processes of *Route 1* and *Route 2*—processes drawn right from the Axioms. Each one is described in detail—*how* the process is used, *why* it works, the axiomatic technology that underlies its use, and the complete explanation of how a being can break the *false agreements* and *self-created barriers* that enslave him to the physical universe. In short, this book contains the ultimate summary of thetan exterior OT ability and its permanent accomplishment.

PHOENIX LECTURES: FREEING THE HUMAN SPIRIT • Here is the panoramic view of Scientology complete. Having codified the subject of Scientology in Creation of Human Ability, Ron then delivered a series of half-hour lectures to specifically accompany a full study of the book. From the *essentials* that underlie the technology—*The Axioms, Conditions of Existence* and *Considerations and Mechanics,* to the processes of *Intensive Procedure,* including twelve lectures describing one-by-one the thetan exterior processes of *Route 1*—it's all covered in full, providing a conceptual understanding of the *science of knowledge* and *native state OT ability.* Here then are the bedrock principles upon which everything in Scientology rests, including the embracive statement of the religion and its heritage—*Scientology, Its General Background.* Hence, this is the watershed lecture series on Scientology itself, and the axiomatic foundation for all future research. *42 lectures.*

DIANETICS 55!—*THE COMPLETE MANUAL OF HUMAN COMMUNICATION* • With all breakthroughs to date, a single factor had been isolated as crucial to success in every type of auditing. As LRH said, "Communication is so thoroughly important today in Dianetics and Scientology (as it always has been on the whole track) that it could be said if you were to get a preclear into communication, you would get him well." And this book delineates the *exact,* but previously unknown, anatomy and formulas for *perfect* communication. The magic of the communication cycle is *the* fundamental of auditing and the primary reason auditing works. The breakthroughs here opened new vistas of application—discoveries of such magnitude, LRH called Dianetics 55! the *Second Book* of Dianetics.

THE UNIFICATION CONGRESS: COMMUNICATION! FREEDOM & ABILITY • The historic Congress announcing the reunification of the subjects of Dianetics and Scientology with the release of *Dianetics 55!* Until now, each had operated in their own sphere: Dianetics addressed Man *as Man*—the first four dynamics, while Scientology addressed *life itself*—the Fifth to Eighth Dynamics. The formula which would serve as the foundation for all future development was contained in a single word: *Communication.* It was a paramount breakthrough Ron would later call, "the great discovery of Dianetics and Scientology." Here, then, are the lectures, as it happened. *16 lectures and accompanying reproductions of the original LRH hand-drawn lecture charts.*

SCIENTOLOGY: THE FUNDAMENTALS OF THOUGHT—*THE BASIC BOOK OF THE THEORY AND PRACTICE OF SCIENTOLOGY FOR BEGINNERS* • Designated by Ron as the *Book One of Scientology*. After having fully unified and codified the subjects of Dianetics and Scientology came the refinement of their *fundamentals*. Originally published as a résumé of Scientology for use in translations into non-English tongues, this book is of inestimable value to both the beginner and advanced student of the mind, spirit and life. Equipped with this book alone, one can begin a practice and perform seeming miracle changes in the states of well-being, ability and intelligence of people. Contained within are the *Conditions of Existence, Eight Dynamics, ARC Triangle, Parts of Man,* the full analysis of *Life as a Game,* and more, including exact processes for individual application of these principles in processing. Here, then, in one book, is the starting point for bringing Scientology to people everywhere.

HUBBARD PROFESSIONAL COURSE LECTURES • While Fundamentals of Thought stands as an introduction to the subject for beginners, it also contains a distillation of fundamentals for every Scientologist. Here are the in-depth descriptions of those fundamentals, each lecture one-half hour in length and providing, one-by-one, a complete mastery of a single Scientology breakthrough—*Axioms 1–10; The Anatomy of Control; Handling of Problems; Start, Change and Stop; Confusion and Stable Data; Exteriorization; Valences* and more—the *why* behind them, *how* they came to be and their mechanics. And it's all brought together with the *Code of a Scientologist*, point by point, and its use in actually creating a new civilization. In short, here are the LRH lectures that make a *Professional Scientologist*—one who can apply the subject to every aspect of life. *21 lectures.*

ADDITIONAL BOOKS CONTAINING SCIENTOLOGY ESSENTIALS

WORK

THE PROBLEMS OF WORK—*SCIENTOLOGY APPLIED TO THE WORKADAY WORLD* •
Having codified the entire subject of Scientology, Ron immediately set out to
provide the *beginning* manual for its application by anyone. As he described it: life
is composed of seven-tenths work, one-tenth familial, one-tenth political and
one-tenth relaxation. Here, then, is Scientology applied to that seven-tenths of
existence including the answers to *Exhaustion* and the *Secret of Efficiency*. Here,
too, is the analysis of life itself—a game composed of exact rules. Know them
and you succeed. Problems of Work contains technology no one can live without,
and that can immediately be applied by both the Scientologist and those new to
the subject.

LIFE PRINCIPLES

SCIENTOLOGY: A NEW SLANT ON LIFE • Scientology essentials for every aspect
of life. Basic answers that put you in charge of your existence, truths to consult
again and again: *Is It Possible to Be Happy?, Two Rules for Happy Living, Personal
Integrity, The Anti-Social Personality* and many more. In every part of this book
you will find Scientology truths that describe conditions in your life and furnish
exact ways to improve them. Scientology: A New Slant on Life contains essential
knowledge for every Scientologist and a perfect introduction for anyone new
to the subject.

AXIOMS, CODES AND SCALES

SCIENTOLOGY 0-8: THE BOOK OF BASICS • The companion to *all* Ron's books,
lectures and materials. This is *the* Book of Basics, containing indispensable data
you will refer to constantly: the *Axioms of Dianetics and Scientology; The Factors;*
a full compilation of all *Scales*—more than 100 in all; listings of the *Perceptics*
and *Awareness Levels;* all *Codes* and *Creeds* and much more. The senior laws of
existence are condensed into this single volume, distilled from more than 15,000
pages of writings, 3,000 lectures and scores of books.

210

$\mathcal{S}$CIENTOLOGY ETHICS: TECHNOLOGY OF OPTIMUM SURVIVAL

INTRODUCTION TO SCIENTOLOGY ETHICS • A new hope for Man arises with the first workable technology of ethics—technology to help an individual pull himself out of the downward skid of life and to a higher plateau of survival. This is the comprehensive handbook providing the crucial fundamentals: *Basics of Ethics & Justice; Honesty; Conditions of Existence; Condition Formulas* from Confusion to Power; the *Basics of Suppression* and its handling; as well as *Justice Procedures* and their use in Scientology Churches. Here, then, is the technology to overcome any barriers in life and in one's personal journey up the Bridge to Total Freedom.

$\mathcal{P}$URIFICATION

CLEAR BODY, CLEAR MIND—*THE EFFECTIVE PURIFICATION PROGRAM* • We live in a biochemical world, and this book is the solution. While investigating the harmful effects that earlier drug use had on preclears' cases, Ron made the major discovery that many street drugs, particularly LSD, remained in a person's body long after ingested. Residues of the drug, he noted, could have serious and lasting effects, including triggering further "trips." Additional research revealed that a wide range of substances—medical drugs, alcohol, pollutants, household chemicals and even food preservatives—could also lodge in the body's tissues. Through research on thousands of cases, he developed the *Purification Program* to eliminate their destructive effects. Clear Body, Clear Mind details every aspect of the all-natural regimen that can free one from the harmful effects of drugs and other toxins, opening the way for spiritual progress.

REFERENCE HANDBOOKS

WHAT IS SCIENTOLOGY?

The complete and essential encyclopedic reference on the subject and practice of Scientology. Organized for use, this book contains the pertinent data on every aspect of the subject:

• The life of L. Ron Hubbard and his path of discovery

• The Spiritual Heritage of the religion

• A full description of Dianetics and Scientology

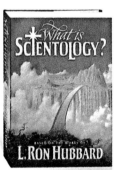

• Auditing—what it is and how it works

• Courses—what they contain and how they are structured

• The Grade Chart of Services and how one ascends to higher states

• The Scientology Ethics and Justice System

• The Organizational Structure of the Church

• A complete description of the many Social Betterment programs supported by the Church, including: Drug Rehabilitation, Criminal Reform, Literacy and Education and the instilling of real values for morality

Over 1,000 pages in length, with more than 500 photographs and illustrations, this text further includes Creeds, Codes, a full listing of all books and materials as well as a Catechism with answers to virtually any question regarding the subject.

You Ask and This Book Answers.

THE SCIENTOLOGY HANDBOOK

Scientology fundamentals for daily use in every part of life. Encompassing 19 separate bodies of technology, here is the most comprehensive manual on the basics of life ever published. Each chapter contains key principles and technology for your continual use:

• Study Technology

• The Dynamics of Existence

• The Components of Understanding— Affinity, Reality and Communication

• The Tone Scale

• Communication and its Formulas

• Assists for Illnesses and Injuries

• How to Resolve Conflicts

• Integrity and Honesty

• Ethics and Condition Formulas

• Answers to Suppression and a Dangerous Environment

• Marriage

• Children

• Tools for the Workplace

More than 700 photographs and illustrations make it easy for you to learn the procedures and apply them at once. This book is truly the indispensable handbook for every Scientologist.

The Technology to Build a Better World.

ABOUT L. RON HUBBARD

"To really know life," L. Ron Hubbard wrote, "you've got to be part of life. You must get down and look, you must get into the nooks and crannies of existence. You have to rub elbows with all kinds and types of men before you can finally establish what he is."

Through his long and extraordinary journey to the founding of Dianetics and Scientology, Ron did just that. From his adventurous youth in a rough and tumble American West to his far-flung trek across a still mysterious Asia; from his two-decade search for the very essence of life to the triumph of Dianetics and Scientology—such are the stories recounted in the L. Ron Hubbard Biographical Publications.

Presenting the photographic overview of Ron's greater journey is *L. Ron Hubbard: Images of a Lifetime.* Drawn from his own archival collection, this is Ron's life as he himself saw it.

While for the many aspects of that rich and varied life, stands the Ron Series. Each issue focuses on a specific LRH profession: *Auditor, Humanitarian, Philosopher, Artist, Poet, Music Maker, Photographer* and many more including his published articles on *Freedom* and his personal *Letters & Journals*. Here is the life of a man who lived at least twenty lives in the space of one.

FOR FURTHER INFORMATION VISIT
www.lronhubbard.org

*G*UIDE TO THE MATERIALS

YOU'RE ON AN ADVENTURE! HERE'S THE MAP.

- All books
- All lectures
- All reference books

All of it laid out in chronological sequence with descriptions of what each contains.

*Y*our journey to a full understanding of Dianetics and Scientology is the greatest adventure of all. But you need a map that shows you where you are and where you are going.

That map is the Materials Guide Chart. It shows all Ron's books and lectures with a full description of their content and subject matter so you can find exactly what *you* are looking for and precisely what *you* need.

Since each book and lecture is laid out in chronological sequence, you can see *how* the subjects of Dianetics and Scientology were developed. And what that means is by simply studying this chart you are in for cognition after cognition!

New editions of all books include extensive glossaries, containing definitions for every technical term. And as a result of a monumental restoration program, the entire library of Ron's lectures are being made available on compact disc, with complete transcripts, glossaries, lecture graphs, diagrams and issues he refers to in the lectures. As a result, you get *all* the data, and can learn with ease, gaining a full *conceptual* understanding.

And what that adds up to is a new Golden Age of Knowledge every Dianeticist and Scientologist has dreamed of.

**To obtain your FREE Materials Guide Chart and Catalog,
or to order L. Ron Hubbard's books and lectures, contact:**

WESTERN HEMISPHERE:
**Bridge
Publications, Inc.**
4751 Fountain Avenue
Los Angeles, CA 90029 USA
www.bridgepub.com
Phone: 1-800-722-1733
Fax: 1-323-953-3328

EASTERN HEMISPHERE:
**New Era Publications
International ApS**
Store Kongensgade 53
1264 Copenhagen K, Denmark
www.newerapublications.com
Phone: (45) 33 73 66 66
Fax: (45) 33 73 66 33

*Books and lectures are also available direct from Churches of Scientology.
See **Addresses**.*

*A*DDRESSES

*D*ianetics is a forerunner and substudy of Scientology, the fastest-growing religion in the world today. Centers and Churches exist in cities throughout the world, and new ones are continually forming.

To obtain more information or to locate the Church or Center nearest you, visit the Scientology website:

www.scientology.org
e-mail: info@scientology.org

or

Phone: 1-800-334-LIFE
(for US and Canada)

You can also write to any one of the Continental Organizations, listed on the following page, who can direct you to one of the thousands of Churches and Centers world over.

L. Ron Hubbard's books and lectures may be obtained from any of these addresses or direct from the publishers on the previous page.

CONTINENTAL CHURCH ORGANIZATIONS:

UNITED STATES

CHURCH OF SCIENTOLOGY
CONTINENTAL LIAISON OFFICE
WESTERN UNITED STATES
1308 L. Ron Hubbard Way
Los Angeles, California 90027 USA
info@wus.scientology.org

CHURCH OF SCIENTOLOGY
CONTINENTAL LIAISON OFFICE
EASTERN UNITED STATES
349 W. 48th Street
New York, New York 10036 USA
info@eus.scientology.org

CANADA

CHURCH OF SCIENTOLOGY
CONTINENTAL LIAISON OFFICE
CANADA
696 Yonge Street, 2nd Floor
Toronto, Ontario
Canada M4Y 2A7
info@scientology.ca

LATIN AMERICA

CHURCH OF SCIENTOLOGY
CONTINENTAL LIAISON OFFICE
LATIN AMERICA
Federacion Mexicana de Dianetica
Calle Puebla #31
Colonia Roma, Mexico D.F.
C.P. 06700, Mexico
info@scientology.org.mx

UNITED KINGDOM

CHURCH OF SCIENTOLOGY
CONTINENTAL LIAISON OFFICE
UNITED KINGDOM
Saint Hill Manor
East Grinstead, West Sussex
England, RH19 4JY
info@scientology.org.uk

AFRICA

CHURCH OF SCIENTOLOGY
CONTINENTAL LIAISON OFFICE AFRICA
5 Cynthia Street
Kensington
Johannesburg 2094, South Africa
info@scientology.org.za

AUSTRALIA, NEW ZEALAND & OCEANIA
CHURCH OF SCIENTOLOGY
CONTINENTAL LIAISON OFFICE ANZO
16 Dorahy Street
Dundas, New South Wales 2117
Australia
info@scientology.org.au

Church of Scientology
Liaison Office of Taiwan
1st, No. 231, Cisian 2nd Road
Kaoshiung City
Taiwan, ROC
info@scientology.org.tw

EUROPE
CHURCH OF SCIENTOLOGY
CONTINENTAL LIAISON OFFICE EUROPE
Store Kongensgade 55
1264 Copenhagen K, Denmark
info@scientology.org.dk

Church of Scientology
Liaison Office of Commonwealth
of Independent States
Management Center of Dianetics
and Scientology Dissemination
Pervomajskaya Street, House 1A
Korpus Grazhdanskoy Oboroni
Losino-Petrovsky Town
141150 Moscow, Russia
info@scientology.ru

Church of Scientology
Liaison Office of Central Europe
1082 Leonardo da Vinci u. 8-14
Budapest, Hungary
info@scientology.hu

Church of Scientology
Liaison Office of Iberia
C/Miguel Menendez Boneta, 18
28460 – Los Molinos
Madrid, Spain
info@spain.scientology.org

Church of Scientology
Liaison Office of Italy
Via Cadorna, 61
20090 Vimodrone
Milan, Italy
info@scientology.it

*B*ECOME A MEMBER
OF THE INTERNATIONAL
ASSOCIATION OF SCIENTOLOGISTS

*T*he International Association of Scientologists is the membership organization of all Scientologists united in the most vital crusade on Earth.

A free Six-Month Introductory Membership is extended to anyone who has not held a membership with the Association before.

As a member, you are eligible for discounts on Scientology materials offered only to IAS Members. You also receive the Association magazine, *IMPACT*, issued six times a year, full of Scientology news from around the world.

The purpose of the IAS is:

"To unite, advance, support and protect Scientology and Scientologists in all parts of the world so as to achieve the Aims of Scientology as originated by L. Ron Hubbard."

Join the strongest force for positive change on the planet today, opening the lives of millions to the greater truth embodied in Scientology.

JOIN THE INTERNATIONAL
ASSOCIATION OF SCIENTOLOGISTS.

To apply for membership,
write to the International
Association of Scientologists
c/o Saint Hill Manor, East Grinstead
West Sussex, England, RH19 4JY

www.iasmembership.org

*E*DITOR'S GLOSSARY
of Words, Terms and Phrases

Words often have several meanings. The definitions used here only give the meaning that the word has as it is used in this book. Dianetics terms appear in bold type. Beside each definition you will find the page on which it first appears, so you can refer back to the text if you wish.

This glossary is not meant to take the place of standard language or Dianetics and Scientology dictionaries, which should be referred to for any words, terms or phrases that do not appear below.

The chapter LRH Glossary should be read, in full, for a proper grounding in the nomenclature of this subject. Definitions from that chapter are, however, included below for ease of reference and are noted where they occur.

—The Editors

AAs: an abbreviation for *attempted abortions.* Page 13.

abdication: renouncing or giving up power, responsibility or the like. Page 114.

abstract(s): pertaining to an idea or term considered apart from what can be sensed, measured or experienced. Page 121.

ACCESSIBILITY: THE STATE OF BEING WILLING TO BE PROCESSED (TECHNICAL SENSE IN THIS SCIENCE). THE STATE OF BEING WILLING TO HAVE INTERPERSONAL RELATIONS (SOCIAL SENSE). FOR THE INDIVIDUAL HIMSELF, ACCESSIBILITY WITH SELF MEANS WHETHER OR NOT AN INDIVIDUAL CAN RECONTACT HIS PAST EXPERIENCES OR DATA. A MAN WITH A "BAD MEMORY" (INTERPOSED BLOCKS BETWEEN CONTROL CENTER AND FACSIMILES) HAS MEMORIES WHICH ARE NOT ACCESSIBLE TO HIM. (From *LRH Glossary.*) Page 26.

account for: 1. to be the cause, agent or source of. Page 153.

2. give a satisfactory reason or explanation for something. Page 153.

ACT: A STAGE OF PROCESSING. APPLIES SOLELY TO THE PARTICULAR PROCESS IN USE AT A CERTAIN CASE LEVEL. (From *LRH Glossary.*) Page 26.

action, course of: a particular manner of proceeding. Also, a chosen path of activity. Page 95.

action phrases: words or phrases in engrams or locks which cause the individual to perform involuntary actions on the time track. See *Science of Survival.* Page 175.

acute: brief or having a short course or occurring occasionally, as opposed to chronic, long-lasting or happening continually. Page 150.

Adam: according to a Biblical account, Adam was the first man. Eve was then created from Adam's rib and given to him by God to be his wife, and they became the parents of the human race. Page 122.

adding machines: machines capable of adding numbers and sometimes other simple arithmetic functions. Such machines were operated manually through large keys which displayed numbers or descriptive words on their surface. One of the keys was labeled "clear" and removed all past computations, allowing the operator a fresh start on a calculation. Page 146.

address: direction of one's attention, skills or energies. Page 3.

adjudication: the act or process of making a formal judgment or decision about something. Page 13.

adz: an axlike tool with a curved, chisel-like steel blade mounted at a right angle to a wooden handle, used for trimming and shaping wood. Page 17.

affair: a thing or matter; something of a particular kind, usually with a descriptive or qualifying term, as in *"a this-lifetime affair."* Page 84.

age flashes: the first impression of age a person receives in answer to the question, "When I snap my fingers, an age will occur to you.

Give me the first number that comes into your mind." Using the flash answer, one will discover at what point on the time track the preclear has most of his attention units. Page 139.

aggregations, colonial: groups of organisms formed together into a connected structure and living or growing in close association with each other. *Colonies* in this sense means groups or masses of individual animals or plants, of the same kind, living or growing in close association. *Aggregation* is used in its biological sense, the act or process of organisms coming together to form a group. Page 174.

ally: a person recorded in the reactive mind of the preclear about whom the preclear makes the reactive computation that this person is necessary to the preclear's survival. Page 29.

anesthesia: without feeling or sensation. Page 79.

anesthetic, general: a drug that produces loss of sensation in the entire body, or in many parts of the body, together with unconsciousness (commonly used for surgical procedures); as opposed to a local anesthetic, affecting a local (particular) area of the body. Page 59.

antagonist: something opposing or in conflict with something else. An *antagonist* is the principal character in opposition (such as a villain) to the *protagonist* or main character or hero of a narrative or drama. Page 21.

apathies: attitudes or feelings of apathy manifested by a lack of feeling or emotion; absences of interest or concern. Page 150.

apologize: make excuse, justification or defense, as for a course of action or behavior. Page 87.

arbitrary: a factor introduced in a problem's solution when that factor does not derive from a known natural law but only from an opinion or authoritarian command. Page 164.

arduous: hard to endure; severe. Page 80.

223

arrivals of the US Cavalry: reference to the mounted soldiers in nineteenth-century America, traditionally portrayed as coming to the rescue of those in danger in the Old West. Page 115.

as in: as regards, with respect or reference to. Page 48.

aspect(s): 1. nature; quality; character, as in *"There are two case aspects."* Page 3.
2. ways in which a thing may be viewed or regarded, as in *"The evolution of Man presents many fascinating aspects, but they have basic simplicities."* Page 22.

assailed: attacked vigorously. Page 121.

assesses: examines (something) in order to judge; determines the significance, importance or value of (something). Page 26.

ASSESSMENT: AN INVENTORY, AN EXAMINATION OR A CALCULATION OR EVALUATION OF A CASE. (From *LRH Glossary.*) Page 27.

ASSISTS: THE STRAIGHT PERCEPTION-BY-PERCEPTION RUNNING, OVER AND OVER, OF AN ACCIDENT OR INCIDENT, UNTIL IT IS DESENSITIZED AS A FACSIMILE AND CANNOT AFFECT THE PRECLEAR. THE ASSIST IS USED IMMEDIATELY AFTER ACCIDENTS OR OPERATIONS. IT TAKES AWAY SHOCK AND MOST OF THE HARMFUL EFFECTS OF THE INCIDENT AND PROMOTES HEALING. IT IS DONE BY STARTING THE INDIVIDUAL AT THE BEGINNING OF THE INCIDENT, WITH THE FIRST AWARENESS OF THE INCIDENT, JUST AS THOUGH THE PRECLEAR WERE LIVING IT ALL THE WAY THROUGH AGAIN WITH FULL PERCEPTION OF SIGHT, SOUND, ETC., AS NEARLY AS THEY CAN BE OBTAINED. AN ASSIST RUN, FOR INSTANCE, IMMEDIATELY AFTER A DENTAL OPERATION TAKES ALL THE SHOCK OUT OF THE OPERATION. ONE CONCLUDES AN ASSIST BY PICKING UP THE AUDITING AS ANOTHER INCIDENT AND RUNNING THROUGH THE AUDITING AND THE DECISION TO BE AUDITED. AN ASSIST SAVES LIVES AND MATERIALLY SPEEDS HEALING. (From *LRH Glossary.*) Page 27.

assume(d): 1. to accept something as existing or being true without proof; suppose, as in *"When in doubt, always assume the preclear is below 2.0."* Page 28.

2. take on a particular state, quality, character or the like, as in *"Running the curve in reverse locates the false supports and identities the preclear has assumed."* Page 115.

3. take upon oneself, as a responsibility, obligation, etc., as in *"Responsibility is the ability and willingness to assume the status of full source and cause."* Page 127.

4. take over or seize something, often that belongs to something or someone else, as in *"assume control."* Page 183.

assumption: 1. the act of taking upon oneself, as a responsibility, obligation, etc. Page 127.

2. the act of taking on (something) as if one's own, as particular characteristics, qualities or the like. Page 186.

astigmatism: a fault in the lens of the eye which reduces the quality of sight, especially a fault which stops the eye from focusing. Page 153.

attend: 1. pay attention; listen to and consider, as in *"Hence, attend!"* Page 113.

2. associated with something or resulting or following from it, as in *"that drop or rise on the Tone Scale attend to failure to control on any dynamic."* Page 113.

at will: just as or when one wishes. Page 115.

AUDITOR: ONE WHO LISTENS AND COMPUTES. A TECHNICIAN OF THIS SCIENCE. (From *LRH Glossary.*) Page 3.

austere: showing strict self-discipline and self-denial. Page 121.

authoritarian: of or having to do with an authority. *Authority* here refers to one who has power to determine, pass judgment, dictate or command without reference to data, facts or observation. Page 164.

automaton: somebody who resembles a machine in their actions or behavior. Page 106.

axioms: statements of natural laws on the order of those of the physical sciences. Page 161.

back off: withdraw or abandon one's actions. Page 36.

balk: that which restrains, hinders or stops something. Page 192.

banded (together): formed or united into a group of things acting or functioning together in a common activity. Page 21.

bawl out: a severe, loud or harsh criticism or scolding. Page 115.

bear: manage to tolerate or endure. Page 99.

Beingness: the state of cause. You are trying to continue to be cause on all dynamics. Cause is "to be," "I am." That is the state of cause. A person goes all through his life trying to be cause. Page 39.

bell tolls, for whom the: a reference to a line from a poem by English poet John Donne (1572–1631), which reads in part: "No man is an island, entire of itself; every man is a piece of the continent, a part of the main … any man's death diminishes me, because I am involved in mankind; and therefore never send to know for whom the bell tolls; it tolls for thee." Historically, church bells have been tolled (rung slowly) to announce deaths. Page 127.

blazed, trail: marked out a path or route; to have set an example by being the first to do something; pioneered. *Blazed* here literally means marked with *blazes,* marks made on a tree by cutting the bark so as to mark a route *(trail).* Page 58.

blow: leave, depart, disappear or go, as if by an explosive action. Page 80.

blueprint, genetic: the plans of construction of a new body (in the orthodox manner of conception, birth and growth). Page 48.

blunt: abrupt; lacking regard for the feelings of others. Page 14.

blunted: weakened or impaired in force; made less effective. Page 74.

bluntly: in a manner that is direct and straightforward. Page 148.

board, wrong side of the: meaning the disadvantageous, undesirable side of some place, object or situation, likened to a game played on a board such as that used for the game of chess. Page 49.

borne in mind: carried in the mind; remembered, as of a fact or piece of information that is important or could be useful in the future. Page 27.

bound: compelled or obligated as a result of a restraining or uniting influence. Page 54.

box top: the very top part of a box containing a commercial product, such as a breakfast cereal, usually bearing the brand name of the product. This is in reference to promotions run to attract consumers where a free gift, prize, etc., is offered in exchange for a designated number of box tops or a certain number of box tops with a small amount of money. To receive the advertised item, the consumer must tear off the box top(s) and send it or "a reasonable facsimile thereof" (an acceptable copy of it) to the manufacturer. Page 148.

bracketed: arranged in brackets, meaning sections of a continuous scale. Page 3.

breaks up: *see* **BROKEN.**

BROKEN: SLANG USED IN THE WISE OF "BREAKING A CASE," MEANING THAT ONE BREAKS THE HOLD OF THE PRECLEAR ON A NON-SURVIVAL FACSIMILE. USED IN GREATER OR LESSER MAGNITUDE, SUCH AS "BREAKING A CIRCUIT" OR "BREAKING INTO A CHAIN" OR "BREAKING A COMPUTATION." NEVER BREAKING THE PRECLEAR OR HIS SPIRIT, BUT BREAKING WHAT IS BREAKING THE PRECLEAR. (From *LRH Glossary.*) Page 26.

building blocks: literally, large blocks of concrete or similar hard material used for building houses and other large structures. Hence, anything thought of as a basic unit of construction such as an element or component regarded as contributing to the growth or development of something. Page 174.

bursitis: inflammation of a bursa, particularly at the elbow, knee or shoulder joint. A *bursa* is a fluid-filled sac that reduces friction around joints or between other parts that rub against one another. Page 153.

but: no more than; only. Page 21.

by all means: in every possible way; without fail; certainly. Page 60.

byproduct(s): 1. incidental (without design or plan) products produced as a result of the making or creating of something else. Page 22.

2. the result of another action, often unintended. Page 121.

by the way: used to introduce something that is not strictly part of the subject at hand; in passing as a side topic. Page 99.

bywords: words or phrases embodying the guiding principles or rules of action of a person, group or time period. Page 120.

called into play: caused or put into operation; caused to come into force or activity. Page 13.

calves, golden: things like the golden calf which, according to the Bible, became an object of worship by Israelites who created it by melting down gold jewelry while Moses was receiving the Ten Commandments from God. Upon his return, Moses made the people destroy the idol. Hence, any false gods or anything worshiped undeservedly. Page 113.

carbon-oxygen motor: a motor (a machine that imparts motion) which operates on carbon and oxygen. The material body of a human is a low-heat engine that runs on a carbon-oxygen system—oxygen from the air and carbon from food are mixed together to form energy. The body runs at 98.6 degrees Fahrenheit (37 centigrade), and the combustion makes it possible for the body to carry out various functions including movement of the muscles. Page 43.

case: a general term for a person being or about to be audited. Page 3.

case: 1. an instance of something; an occurrence; an example, as in *"In the case of psychotics, the Second, Third and Fourth Acts may be changed in their order."* Page 26.

2. the actual state of things, as in *"At 1.1, single source looks to be the case."* Page 122.

case, in any: whatever the circumstances may be; regardless of what has occurred or will occur. Page 9.

catalyze: increase the rate of a chemical reaction. Page 43.

catalyzed: driven or urged into action, as by reaction to a stimulus. Page 152.

Cavalry, arrivals of the US: reference to the mounted soldiers in nineteenth-century America, traditionally portrayed as coming to the rescue of those in danger in the Old West. Page 115.

cell(s): the smallest structural unit of an organism that is capable of independent functioning. All plants and animals are made up materially of one or more cells that usually combine to form various tissues. For instance the human body has more than 10 trillion cells. Page 21.

cell, original: a reference to the theory that life forms began in a primitive ocean when supposedly spontaneous events created a single cell capable of reproducing other cells and hence, life forms. Page 122.

cellular: having to do with a *cell*, the smallest structural unit of an organism that is capable of independent functioning. All plants and animals are made up materially of one or more cells that usually combine to form various tissues. For instance the human body has more than 10 trillion cells. Page 21.

cellular colony: a group or mass of cells. *Cellular* means having to do with a *cell*, the smallest structural unit of an organism that is capable of independent functioning. *Colony* in this sense means groups or masses of individual animals or plants, of the same kind, living or growing in close association. Page 21.

CENTER OF CONTROL: THE AWARENESS OF AWARENESS UNIT OF THE MIND. THIS IS NOT PART OF THE BRAIN, BUT PART OF THE MIND, THE BRAIN BEING PHYSIOLOGICAL. THE MIND HAS

TWO CONTROL CENTERS POSSIBLE, BY DEFINITION, THE RIGHT AND THE LEFT. ONE IS AN ACTUAL GENETIC CONTROL CENTER. THE OTHER IS A SUB-CONTROL CENTER, SUBSERVIENT TO THE CONTROL CENTER. (From *LRH Glossary*.) Page 22.

chemical heat engine: a reference to the body of a living organism which converts chemical energy (from food or other fuel) into heat and provides mechanical energy, such as to move the body's muscles. Page 171.

chronic: long-lasting or happening continually, as of an illness, medical condition, etc. Page 28.

circuit: a pseudo-personality (false personality) out of a facsimile strong enough to dictate to the individual and BE the individual. See *Dianetics: The Modern Science of Mental Health.* Page 75.

clairvoyants: persons with *clairvoyance,* the power of seeing objects or events beyond the range of natural vision. Page 29.

CLEAR: *(VERB)* THE ACT OF DESENSITIZING OR RELEASING A THOUGHT IMPRESSION OR A SERIES OF IMPRESSIONS OR OBSERVATIONS IN THE PAST OR A POSTULATE OR AN EMOTION OR AN EFFORT OR AN ENTIRE FACSIMILE. THE PRECLEAR EITHER RELEASES HIS HOLD ON THE FACSIMILE (MEMORY) OR THE FACSIMILE ITSELF IS DESENSITIZED. THE WORD IS TAKEN FROM ELECTRONIC COMPUTERS OR COMMON OFFICE ADDING MACHINES AND DESCRIBES AN ACTION SIMILAR TO CLEARING PAST COMPUTATIONS FROM THE MACHINES. (From *LRH Glossary*.) Page 25.

CLEAR: *(NOUN)* A MUCH MISUNDERSTOOD STATE OF BEING. THE WORD HAS BEEN USED BEFORE WITH OTHER MEANINGS. IT HAS BEEN MISTAKEN AS AN ABSOLUTE. IT IS STILL USED. IT IS USED HERE AS ELECTRONICS SLANG AND CAN APPLY TO A CHAIN, AN INCIDENT OR A COMPUTATION. (From *LRH Glossary*.)

cohesion: the act or state of *cohering,* uniting or sticking together; figuratively, a nonmaterial union. Page 184.

colonial aggregations: groups of organisms formed together into a connected structure and living or growing in close association with each other. *Colonies* in this sense means groups or masses of individual animals or plants, of the same kind, living or growing in close association. *Aggregation* is used in its biological sense, the act or process of organisms coming together to form a group. Page 174.

combustion: the process of burning something. Specifically in chemistry, the chemical combination of a substance with oxygen, involving the release of energy and/or heat for the production of power, such as in the human body to move muscles or to carry out cell maintenance and growth. (In the human body, oxygen from the air and carbon from food mixed together produce heat and energy.) Page 43.

come to light: to become known. Page 54.

commingle: mingle or mix together. Page 122.

common denominator: something common to or characteristic of a number of people, things, situations, etc.; a shared characteristic. Page 128.

comparable magnitude: *comparable* means capable of being compared; having features in common with something else to permit or suggest comparison. *Magnitude* means relative size, amount, importance, extent or influence. A datum can be evaluated only by a datum of comparable magnitude. Page 163.

complex compounds: *see* **compound(s)**.

compound(s): substances containing two or more elements (substances that themselves cannot be broken down into simpler substances) in exact proportions. Each compound has its own distinctive properties. Compounds may be solids, liquids or gases. Living things have the ability to add compounds together to form *complex compounds* such as found in the cells of the body. Page 129.

compounded: produced, created or formed by combining two or more things, items, elements, etc. Page 83.

compound word: a word made up of two or more other words. For example, teapot, from *tea* and *pot* or blackbird, from *black* and *bird*. MEST is a compound word made up from (the first letters) of four other words: *matter, energy, space* and *time*. Page 156.

computation: technically, is that aberrated evaluation and postulate that one must be consistently in a certain state in order to succeed. The computation thus may mean that one must "entertain in order to be alive" or that one must "be dignified in order to succeed" or that one must "own much in order to live." Computations are fully described in the chapter *Computations*. Page 3.

computation: the action or result of calculating or processing data (to come up with answers); thinking. Page 9.

computing: *see* **COMPUTING PSYCHOTIC.**

COMPUTING PSYCHOTIC: ONE WHO IS RUNNING ON A CIRCUIT, A CIRCUIT BEING A PSEUDO-PERSONALITY OUT OF A FACSIMILE STRONG ENOUGH TO DICTATE TO THE INDIVIDUAL AND *BE* THE INDIVIDUAL. (From *LRH Glossary*.) Page 3.

confessional: the act of disclosing in private one's sins to a Catholic priest and receiving forgiveness for them. Page 99.

consists in: exists in; lies or resides in. Page 178.

constitute: to be equivalent in effect or value to; have the form or characteristic of (a specified thing). Page 178.

contacted: established a connection, communication or the like (through the mind). Page 69.

control center: (same as *center of control*) THE AWARENESS OF AWARENESS UNIT OF THE MIND. THIS IS NOT PART OF THE BRAIN, BUT PART OF THE MIND, THE BRAIN BEING PHYSIOLOGICAL. THE MIND HAS TWO CONTROL CENTERS POSSIBLE, BY DEFINITION, THE RIGHT AND THE LEFT. ONE IS AN ACTUAL GENETIC CONTROL CENTER. THE OTHER IS A

SUB-CONTROL CENTER, SUBSERVIENT TO THE CONTROL CENTER. (From *LRH Glossary*.) Also, see Axiom 125 in the chapter *Definitions, Logics and Axioms*. Page 21.

conversely: in a way that is reversed, as in position, order or action, yet implying a connection or linked relationship. Page 27.

converters: organisms such as algae that convert units of light from the Sun and minerals from the sea into energy they need to survive. In Axiom 16, *"Organisms can exist only as higher levels of complexities because lower levels of converters exist"* refers to the fact that the largest animals, unable to live on soil and sunlight, live on vegetable forms which are themselves the converters of soil and sunlight into comestibles (things which can be eaten as food) for higher forms. (*Algae* are any of several simple plantlike organisms having no true root, stem or leaf and which use the energy of sunlight to make their own food.) Page 58.

corollary: a proposition that follows upon one just demonstrated and that requires no additional proof. For an example, see Logic 3 in the chapter *Definitions, Logics and Axioms*. Page 162.

cosmic rays: electrically charged, high-energy particles of great penetrating power, that travel through space, such as those emitted from an exploding sun or star, and which reach the Earth. *Cosmic* means of or relating to the universe, especially as distinct from Earth. Page 21.

COUNTER-EFFORT: THE INDIVIDUAL'S OWN EFFORT IS SIMPLY CALLED *EFFORT*. THE EFFORTS OF THE ENVIRONMENT ARE CALLED *COUNTER-EFFORTS*. (From *LRH Glossary*.) *see also* **EFFORT.** Page 9.

counterfeit: of, or pertaining to, giving a false appearance of. Page 116.

course(s): a route, direction, action or series of actions. Page 10.

course of action: a particular manner of proceeding. Also, a chosen path of activity. Page 95.

crass: lacking sensitivity or refinement. Page 14.

criminology: the scientific study of crime, criminals, criminal behavior, punishment and correction. (A *crime* is any illegal act, one forbidden by law, or a failure to act as required by law.) Page 166.

cult: great or excessive devotion or dedication to some person, idea or thing. Page 75.

cycle: a single complete execution of a periodically repeated occurrence. Page 10.

death efforts: the efforts at past deaths, normally violent deaths as opposed to deaths by natural causes. Page 48.

deduced: reasoned or figured out by drawing conclusions from general principles or ideas assumed as true as a basis for further investigation or development of ideas. For example, if one accepts that "all apples are sweet" and one comes across an apple, then one might conclude that this apple is sweet as the basis for further reasoning or confirmation. *See also* **induced.** Page 165.

desensitized: made less forceful or capable of impact. Page 40.

devotion: great dedication and loyalty; enthusiasm for an activity. Page 30.

diffuse: spread out in space; spread through or over a wide area; not concentrated. Page 56.

discharges: relieves of charge (Anger, Fear, Grief or Apathy); unburdens. Page 115.

drained: flowed out or taken out of something (gradually), likened to a liquid flowing out from a container. Page 79.

dramatizations: the duplications of engramic contents, entire or in part, by an aberree (aberrated person) in his present time environment. Aberrated conduct is entirely dramatization. Aberrated conduct will occur only when and if an engram exists in the reactive mind of the aberree. That conduct will be a duplication of such an engram. Page 3.

DRAMATIZING PSYCHOTIC: ONE WHO DRAMATIZES ONE TYPE OF FACSIMILE ONLY. (From *LRH Glossary.*) Page 3.

dream therapy: a form of psychoanalysis created by Sigmund Freud in which dreams are interpreted for their hidden content or symbols, supposedly expressing aspects of the patient's problems. Page 80.

drops away: swiftly declines or decreases, as in quality, quantity or intensity, likened to disappearing from a place, location, condition, etc. Page 55.

dub-in: a term used to characterize vision or recall which is imaginary. The term comes from the motion-picture industry. To "dub," in moviemaking, is to create and add sounds to a picture after filming is complete. This process ("dubbing") results in a fabricated soundtrack that *seems* to the audience like it actually took place when filmed, but much or *all* of it was created in the studio long after filming was finished and then "dubbed in." Hence, "dub-in" is something put there that seems like it happened, but in reality it did not. Page 131.

dwelt upon: spent (much) time on or lingered over (a thing) in action or thought; remained with the attention fixed on. Page 101.

dynamic: from the Greek *dunamikos,* powerful. Hence, motivating or energizing force (of existence or life). Page 168.

DYNAMICS: THE CENTRAL DRIVES OF AN INDIVIDUAL. THEY ARE NUMBERED FROM ONE TO EIGHT AS FOLLOWS: (1) SELF SURVIVAL; (2) SURVIVAL THROUGH CHILDREN (INCLUDES SEXUAL ACT); (3) SURVIVAL BY GROUPS INCLUDING SOCIAL AND POLITICAL AS WELL AS COMMERCIAL; (4) SURVIVAL THROUGH MANKIND AS A WHOLE; (5) SURVIVAL THROUGH LIFE INCLUDING ANY SPECIES, VEGETABLE OR ANIMAL; (6) SURVIVAL THROUGH *MEST;* (7) SURVIVAL THROUGH THETA OR THE STATIC ITSELF; (8) (WRITTEN AS INFINITY—∞) SURVIVAL THROUGH A SUPREME BEING. EACH INDIVIDUAL IS SURVIVING FOR ALL EIGHT. (From *LRH Glossary.*) Page 7.

echelons: levels, as in a steplike arrangement or order. An *echelon* is one of a series in a field of activity. Page 27.

effected: made the effect of. Page 54.

effected: brought about; accomplished; made happen. Page 105.

EFFORT: THE PHYSICAL-FORCE MANIFESTATION OF MOTION. A SHARP EFFORT AGAINST AN INDIVIDUAL PRODUCES PAIN. A STRENUOUS EFFORT PRODUCES DISCOMFORT. EFFORT CAN BE RECALLED AND RE-EXPERIENCED BY THE PRECLEAR. NO PRECLEAR BELOW 2.0 SHOULD BE CALLED UPON TO USE EFFORT AS SUCH, AS HE IS INCAPABLE OF HANDLING IT AND WILL STICK IN IT. THE ESSENTIAL PART OF A PAINFUL FACSIMILE IS ITS EFFORT, NOT ITS PERCEPTIONS. (From *LRH Glossary.*) Page 3.

Effort: shortened form of Effort Processing. *See* **EFFORT PROCESSING.** Page 28.

EFFORT PROCESSING: EFFORT PROCESSING IS DONE BY RUNNING MOMENTS OF PHYSICAL STRESS. THESE ARE RUN EITHER AS SIMPLE EFFORTS OR COUNTER-EFFORTS OR AS WHOLE PRECISE INCIDENTS. SUCH INCIDENTS AS THOSE WHICH CONTAIN PHYSICAL PAIN OR HEAVY STRESS OF MOTION (SUCH AS INJURIES, ACCIDENTS OR ILLNESSES) ARE ADDRESSED BY EFFORT PROCESSING. (From *LRH Glossary.*) Page 30.

elements, the: the four substances, earth, air, fire or water, formerly regarded as fundamental to the makeup of the physical universe. Page 22.

elucidation: the act of explaining or giving a detailed statement of. Page 161.

EMOTION: THE CATALYST USED BY THE CONTROL CENTER TO MONITOR PHYSICAL ACTION. THE RELAY SYSTEM, VIA GLANDS, INTERPOSED BETWEEN "I" AND SELF AND, BY THOUGHT, OTHERS. THE MAIN EMOTIONS ARE HAPPINESS IN WHICH ONE HAS CONFIDENCE AND ENJOYMENT IN HIS GOALS AND A BELIEF IN HIS CONTROL OF ENVIRONMENT; BOREDOM IN WHICH ONE HAS LOST CONFIDENCE AND DIRECTION BUT IS NOT DEFEATED; ANTAGONISM WHEREIN ONE FEELS HIS CONTROL

THREATENED; ANGER WHEREIN ONE SEEKS TO DESTROY THAT
WHICH THREATENS AND SEEKS WITHOUT GOOD DIRECTION
BEYOND DESTRUCTION; COVERT HOSTILITY WHEREIN ONE
SEEKS TO DESTROY WHILE REASSURING HIS TARGET THAT HE IS
NOT SO SEEKING; FEAR WHEREIN ONE IS CATALYZED TO FLEE;
GRIEF IN WHICH ONE RECOGNIZES LOSS; APATHY IN WHICH ONE
ACCEPTS FAILURE ON ALL DYNAMICS AND PRETENDS DEATH.
OTHER EMOTIONS ARE A VOLUME OR LACK OF VOLUME OF
THOSE NAMED. SHAME OR EMBARRASSMENT ARE EMOTIONS
PECULIAR TO GROUPS OR INTERPERSONAL RELATIONS AND ARE
ON A LEVEL WITH GRIEF, DENOTING LOSS OF POSITION IN A
GROUP. EMOTION IS THE GLANDULAR SYSTEM PARALLEL OF
MOTION AND EACH EMOTION REFLECTS ACTION TO GAIN OR
LOSE MOTION. AT A HIGH LEVEL, ONE IS SENDING BACK MOTION;
AT A MID LEVEL, ONE IS HOLDING MOTION; AT A LOWER LEVEL,
MOTION IS SWEEPING THROUGH AND OVER ONE. (From *LRH Glossary*.)
Page 3.

EMOTIONAL CURVE: THE DROP FROM ANY POSITION (ON THE
TONE SCALE) ABOVE 2.0 TO A POSITION BELOW 2.0 ON THE
REALIZATION OF FAILURE OR INADEQUACY. IT IS EASILY
RECOVERED BY PRECLEARS. (From *LRH Glossary*.) Page 3.

Emotion Processing: Emotion Processing is done by Straightwire,
Lock Scanning and Lock and Engram and Secondary Running,
with the total address to emotion. A moment of sympathy, of
determinism, of defiance, of agreement, is run just as though the
incident were an engram—which is to say, the preclear is made
to re-experience the emotion and, incidentally, a few perceptics,
over and over from beginning to end until the emotion is off the
lock. Page 9.

end, an: what is intended or meant to be achieved; object; purpose;
goal. Page 60.

endocrine: having to do with the secretion of chemical substances (hormones) from certain organs and tissues which travel through the blood to all parts of the body. After a hormone arrives at the organ or tissue it affects, it causes certain actions to occur. Hormones regulate such body processes as growth, development, reproduction, response to stress, etc. Page 27.

end (of), to the: to the result or outcome; for the purpose. Page 25.

endowed: (of qualities, abilities or characteristics) provided, supplied, given or equipped with. Page 180.

endowment: power, ability, capacity or other advantage which a person naturally has or is given. Page 171.

end, to this: for this purpose; for this reason. Page 28.

engagement: a promise or agreement to be at a particular place at a particular time. Page 64.

engaging upon: occupying or involving (itself) with; taking part in doing some activity. Page 174.

engrams: *see* **HEAVY FACSIMILE.**

enrandomed: caused to be in the state or condition of being random, without pattern or plan. Page 188.

en route: on or along the way. Page 145.

entheta: a compound word meaning "enturbulated theta," theta in a turbulent state, agitated or disturbed. Page 140.

entity: something that exists separately from other things and has its own identity. Page 95.

environ: environment; surroundings. Page 7.

ENVIRONMENT: THE SURROUNDINGS OF THE PRECLEAR FROM MOMENT TO MOMENT, IN PARTICULAR OR IN GENERAL, INCLUDING PEOPLE, PETS, MECHANICAL OBJECTS, WEATHER, CULTURE, CLOTHING OR THE SUPREME BEING. ANYTHING HE PERCEIVES OR BELIEVES HE PERCEIVES. THE OBJECTIVE ENVIRONMENT IS THE ENVIRONMENT EVERYONE AGREES IS

THERE. THE SUBJECTIVE ENVIRONMENT IS THE ENVIRONMENT THE INDIVIDUAL HIMSELF BELIEVES IS THERE. THEY MAY NOT AGREE. (From *LRH Glossary*.) Page 7.

erased: removed or eliminated completely. Page 29.

ESP: extrasensory perception; perception or communication outside of normal sensory capability. Page 121.

essence: 1. the most important and basic idea, thing, etc. Page 31.
2. a fundamental or most important property of a thing; a quality which determines something's character. Page 84.

essence, in: by its nature; fundamentally. Page 106.

esteemed: regarded highly or favorably; looked upon with respect or admiration. Page 75.

ever afterwards: throughout all the time after a specified date; from that time onward. Page 9.

evidence, out of: not visible, present or conspicuous. Page 30.

evolutionary: having to do with the development of a species or other group through time and the changes that occur within that species or group. Page 22.

exclamation point: literally, a symbol (!) that primarily indicates that a preceding word, phrase or sentence shows strong emotion, such as anger, disbelief, upset, pain, etc. Used figuratively. Page 114.

exert: 1. put forth or put out; put into effect. Page 8.
2. to apply (oneself) with great energy. Page 59.
3. put (oneself) into action; set in operation; make effective; exercise influence. Page 172.

exhaust: draw out or drain off so as to empty completely. Page 9.

extensionally: *extend* means to stretch out or reach (to the fullest extent). In regards to theta, it means exerting itself not through physical application of the organism but through such means as language, ideas, etc. Page 172.

extrapolation: the action of inferring (an unknown) from something that is known. Page 129.

extroverted: having one's interest and attention outward or to things outside the self, as opposed to *introverted,* which is having one's interest and attention inward or to things within oneself. Page 73.

FACSIMILES: A FACSIMILE IS A MEMORY RECORDING FOR A FINITE PERIOD OF TIME. IT IS CONSIDERED THAT MEMORY IS A STATIC WITHOUT WAVELENGTH, WEIGHT, MASS OR POSITION IN SPACE (IN OTHER WORDS, A TRUE STATIC) WHICH YET RECEIVES THE IMPRESSION OF TIME, SPACE, ENERGY AND MATTER. A CAREFUL EXAMINATION OF THE PHENOMENA OF THOUGHT AND THE BEHAVIOR OF THE HUMAN MIND LEADS ONE TO THIS CONCLUSION. THE CONCLUSION IS ITSELF A POSTULATE, USED BECAUSE IT IS EXTREMELY USEFUL AND WORKABLE. THIS IS A POINT OF ECHELON IN RESEARCH THAT A FACSIMILE CAN BE SO DESCRIBED. THE DESCRIPTION IS MATHEMATICAL AND AN ABSTRACT AND MAY OR MAY NOT BE ACTUAL. WHEN A THOUGHT RECORDING IS SO REGARDED, THE PROBLEMS OF THE MIND RAPIDLY RESOLVE. FACSIMILES ARE SAID TO BE "STORED." THEY ACT UPON THE PHYSICAL UNIVERSE SWITCHBOARD, CALLED THE BRAIN AND NERVOUS AND GLANDULAR SYSTEM, TO MONITOR ACTION. THEY APPEAR TO HAVE MOTION AND WEIGHT ONLY BECAUSE MOTION AND WEIGHT ARE RECORDED INTO THEM. THEY ARE NOT STORED IN THE CELLS. THEY IMPINGE UPON THE CELLS. PROOF OF THIS MATTER RESTS IN THE FACT THAT AN ENERGY WHICH BECAME A FACSIMILE A LONG TIME AGO CAN BE RECONTACTED AND IS FOUND TO BE VIOLENT ON THE CONTACT. PAIN IS STORED AS A FACSIMILE. OLD PAIN CAN BE RECONTACTED. OLD PAIN IN FACSIMILE FORM, OLD EMOTION IN FACSIMILE FORM, CAN REIMPOSE ITSELF ON PRESENT TIME IN SUCH A WISE AS TO DEFORM OR OTHERWISE PHYSICALLY EFFECT THE BODY. YOU CAN GO BACK TO THE LAST TIME YOU HURT YOURSELF AND FIND THERE AND RE-EXPERIENCE THE

PAIN OF THAT HURT UNLESS YOU ARE VERY OCCLUDED. YOU CAN RECOVER EFFORTS AND EXERTIONS YOU HAVE MADE OR WHICH HAVE BEEN MADE AGAINST YOU IN THE PAST. YET THE CELLS THEMSELVES, WHICH HAVE FINITE LIFE, ARE LONG SINCE REPLACED ALTHOUGH THE BODY GOES ON. HENCE, THE FACSIMILE THEORY. THE WORD FACSIMILE IS USED, AS BLUNTLY AS ONE USES IT, IN CONNECTION WITH A DRAWING OF A BOX TOP INSTEAD OF THE ACTUAL BOX TOP. IT MEANS A SIMILAR ARTICLE RATHER THAN THE ARTICLE ITSELF. YOU CAN RECALL A MEMORY PICTURE OF AN ELEPHANT OR A PHOTOGRAPH. THE ELEPHANT AND THE PHOTOGRAPH ARE NO LONGER PRESENT. A FACSIMILE OF THEM IS STORED IN YOUR MIND. A FACSIMILE IS COMPLETE WITH EVERY PERCEPTION OF THE ENVIRONMENT PRESENT WHEN THAT FACSIMILE WAS MADE, INCLUDING SIGHT, SOUND, SMELL, TASTE, WEIGHT, JOINT POSITION AND SO ON THROUGH HALF A HUNDRED PERCEPTIONS. JUST BECAUSE YOU CANNOT RECALL MOTION OR THESE PERCEPTIONS DOES NOT MEAN THEY WERE NOT RECORDED FULLY AND IN MOTION WITH EVERY PERCEPTION CHANNEL YOU HAD AT THE TIME. IT DOES MEAN THAT YOU HAVE INTERPOSED A STOP BETWEEN THE FACSIMILE AND THE RECALL MECHANISMS OF YOUR CONTROL CENTERS. THERE ARE FACSIMILES OF EVERYTHING YOU HAVE EXPERIENCED IN YOUR ENTIRE LIFETIME AND EVERYTHING YOU HAVE IMAGINED. (From *LRH Glossary*.) Page 13.

fairly: distinctly and definitely; clearly; fully and actually. Page 116.

Faith: a static of pure theta. In a complete static, there is no understanding. One accepts it. One doesn't try to wonder about it. Page 120.

Faith, Have: the obedience to, acceptance of or belief in something as true without having complete evidence; understanding of, or trust in, something. Page 120.

fall(s) away: gradually weaken in intensity; fade away. Page 10.

fashion, in some: in some manner; in some way. Page 79.

fetish: an object regarded or worshiped with awe or irrational devotion. Page 80.

FIFTEEN: *(NOUN)* A DESIGNATION TO DENOTE A FINISHED CASE. SOLELY FOR CASE RECORDING TO DESIGNATE A CASE ADVANCED TO CURRENT COMPLETION. THIS IS A FOUNDATION NUMBER SYSTEM FOR PRECLEARS. A CASE IS NOTED ON RECORD BY THE ACT NUMBER TO WHICH IT HAS BEEN ADVANCED. (From *LRH Glossary.*) Page 30.

finer: marked by precision of method or technique; precise and exact. Page 9.

5.0: about the highest level of happiness or cheerfulness you could reach. Page 3.

flight: a (swift) passage or movement. Page 114.

following out: pursuing to a conclusion; bringing to a completion or final result. Page 26.

for one thing: used to introduce or refer to one of two or more reasons for saying or doing something. Page 121.

forsakes: gives up, parts with or surrenders. Page 122.

for the most part: in general; on the whole; to the greater extent; mostly. Page 161.

forthright: straightforward or direct; proceeding in a straight course. Page 13.

for whom the bell tolls: a reference to a line from a poem by English poet John Donne (1572–1631), which reads in part: "No man is an island, entire of itself; every man is a piece of the continent, a part of the main ... any man's death diminishes me, because I am involved in mankind; and therefore never send to know for whom the bell tolls; it tolls for thee." Historically, church bells have been tolled (rung slowly) to announce deaths. Page 127.

Foundation: a reference to the Hubbard Dianetics Foundation in Wichita, Kansas, that offered processing and auditor training to public and staff in the early 1950s. From the word *foundation,* as it is the foundation for a new world and a better life. Page 145.

game animal: an animal, such as a deer or rabbit, hunted for sport or food. *Game* in this sense means wild animals, including birds or fish that are hunted for food or pleasure. Page 29.

game bird: any bird hunted for sport or food. *Game* in this sense means wild animals, including birds or fish that are hunted for food or pleasure. Page 29.

Geiger counter: an instrument that detects and measures *radioactivity,* energy emitted in the form of streams of particles. Page 17.

general anesthetic: a drug that produces loss of sensation in the entire body, or in many parts of the body, together with unconsciousness (commonly used for surgical procedures); as opposed to a local anesthetic, affecting a local (particular) area of the body. Page 59.

GENETIC: BY LINE OF PROTOPLASM AND BY FACSIMILES AND BY MEST FORMS, THE INDIVIDUAL HAS ARRIVED IN THE PRESENT AGE FROM A PAST BEGINNING. GENETIC APPLIES TO THE PROTOPLASM LINE OF FATHER AND MOTHER TO CHILD, GROWN CHILD TO NEW CHILD AND SO FORTH. (From *LRH Glossary.*) Page 28.

genetic blueprint: the plans of construction of a new body (in the orthodox manner of conception, birth and growth). Page 48.

genetic line: the evolution of organisms themselves continuing from generation to generation; the evolutionary chain. Page 39.

get out of (something): avoid; escape from; be excused from. Page 10.

getting up: bringing forth into view. Page 14.

given: 1. imparted or communicated; presented (a quality), as in *"has given false value to."* Page 115.

2. stated, fixed or specified, as in *"at a given moment in time."* Page 173.

glandular: consisting of, containing or bearing glands (a cell, group of cells or organ producing a secretion for use elsewhere in the body or for elimination from the body). For example, adrenal glands produce adrenaline, a hormone that is released into the bloodstream in response to physical or mental stress, as from fear of injury. It initiates many bodily responses, including stimulation of heart action and increase in blood pressure. Page 148.

Goal Processing: processing which handles the fact that the reason an individual cannot approach a future goal or even strongly postulate one lies in his inability to resolve the present or to make a decision in the past. Goal Processing is fully described in the chapter *Future Goals*. Page 40.

golden calves: things like the golden calf which, according to the Bible, became an object of worship by Israelites who created it by melting down gold jewelry while Moses was receiving the Ten Commandments from God. Upon his return, Moses made the people destroy the idol. Hence, any false gods or anything worshiped undeservedly. Page 113.

gradient scale: the term *gradient scale* can apply to anything and means a scale of condition graduated from zero to infinity. Absolutes are considered to be unobtainable. Depending on the direction the scale is graduated, there could be an infinity of wrongness and an infinity of rightness. Thus the gradient scale of rightness would run from the theoretical but unobtainable zero of rightness, up to the theoretical infinity of rightness. A gradient scale of wrongness would run from a zero of wrongness to an infinity of wrongness. The word *gradient* is meant to define lessening or increasing degrees of condition. The difference between one point on a gradient scale and another point could be as different or as wide as the entire range of the scale itself, or it could be as tiny as to need the most minute discernment (ability to perceive the difference) for its establishment. Page 120.

grossest: most noticeable or obvious, not fine and subtle. Also, physically large; bulky. Page 21.

hands of, at the: by or through the action of. Page 127.

hang up: to become halted or suspended in one's progress. Page 60.

happenstance: a chance happening or event. Page 130.

heart: the most important and essential part; essence. Page 88.

heavy effort facsimile: *see* **HEAVY FACSIMILE.**

HEAVY FACSIMILE: A HEAVY FACSIMILE USED TO BE KNOWN AS AN "ENGRAM." IN VIEW OF THE FACT THAT IT HAS BEEN FOUND TO BE STORED ELSEWHERE THAN IN THE CELLS, THE TERM "HEAVY FACSIMILE" HAS NOW COME INTO USE. A HEAVY FACSIMILE IS AN EXPERIENCE, COMPLETE WITH ALL PERCEPTIONS AND EMOTIONS AND THOUGHTS AND EFFORTS, OCCUPYING A PRECISE PLACE IN SPACE AND A MOMENT IN TIME. IT CAN BE AN OPERATION, AN INJURY, A TERM OF HEAVY PHYSICAL EXERTION OR EVEN A DEATH. IT IS COMPOSED OF THE PRECLEAR'S OWN EFFORT AND THE EFFORT OF THE ENVIRONMENT (COUNTER-EFFORT). (From *LRH Glossary.*) Page 55.

held in place: kept or maintained in a particular location, position, condition, etc. Page 55.

highest common denominator: the highest in level, rank, quality, kind, etc., of common denominator. A *common denominator* is something common to or characteristic of a number of people, things, situations, etc.; a shared characteristic. Page 128.

high-tone: high on the Tone Scale. Page 3.

hitherto: up to this time; until now. Page 22.

hocus-pocus: meaningless or nonsense talk used for trickery or deception. Page 120.

Homo novis: new man; from the Latin words *homo* (man) and *novus* (new). Page 14.

human novis: same as *Homo novis*, new man. Page 100.

hung up: halted or snagged. Page 106.

hysterical deafness: *hysterical* (of hysteria) describes physical symptoms such as blindness, deafness, paralysis or tremors when no physical cause can be found. A person with a mild case of "hysterical" deafness is one who has difficulty in hearing. This person has something he is afraid to hear. He plays the radio very loudly, makes people repeat continually and misses pieces of the conversation. People are "hysterically" deaf without any conscious knowledge of it. Their "hearing just isn't so good." Page 88.

if only: even if nothing or nowhere else. Page 130.

ills: sicknesses or diseases. Page 153.

imbued: filled with so as to contain or spread throughout, as a particular quality. Page 175.

impresses: through pressure or contact, makes a mark upon any surface, especially by the application of some kind of device such as a stamp, seal, etc. Hence, an effect produced by external force or influence on the mind. Page 188.

in any case: whatever the circumstances may be; regardless of what has occurred or will occur. Page 9.

incident to: accompanying something or occurring as a consequence of it. Page 83.

incursion: the act of entering in or running against; entrance into or invasion of a place, territory, area, sphere of operation, etc. Page 170.

index: 1. something used or serving to point out; an indicator, sign or measure of something. Page 43.

2. something that serves to act as a reference. Page 189.

individuation: the action or process of becoming more and more individual. Page 83.

indoctrinate: cause to accept a set of beliefs uncritically through repeated instruction. Page 113.

induced: reasoned or figured out by starting from particular experiences and facts and proceeding to general laws or principles.

For example, if many apples are tasted and all are sweet, one could conclude all apples are sweet as the basis for further reasoning or confirmation. *See also* **deduced**. Page 165.

in essence: by its nature; fundamentally. Page 106.

inexorable: unyielding, unalterable, inflexible. Page 17.

inextricable: incapable of being pulled apart from each other; that cannot be separated out, one from another. Page 193.

infinity-valued logic: logic could best be explained in terms of an infinity of values. From the theoretical but unobtainable ABSOLUTE WRONG, solutions can be graded through a theoretical midpoint of neither right nor wrong to a theoretical but unobtainable ABSOLUTE RIGHT. Page 163.

in order to: as a means to; with the purpose of. Page 9.

in other words: put differently; otherwise stated, often used to introduce an explanation of something and usually in a simpler way. Page 39.

in particular: especially or specifically. Page 29.

in short: introducing a summary statement in a few words of what has been previously stated; in summary. Page 28.

insidious: acting harmfully in a way that is hidden or hard to distinguish. Page 84.

in some fashion: in some manner; in some way. Page 79.

in store: put away, keep or accumulate in a separate place, as if for future use. Page 47.

interbody: between the parts of a body. *Inter-* means between or among. Page 157.

intercellular: between or among cells. A *cell* is the smallest structural unit of an organism that is capable of independent functioning. Page 21.

interpersonal relations: related to or involving personal and social interactions between people. *Interpersonal* means relating to, occurring among or involving several people. Page 21.

interposed: inserted, introduced or placed between one thing and another. Page 10.

in the main: in most cases; generally; usually. Page 122.

intimately: in a way that involves or brings about a very close connection or union of parts. Page 54.

introverted: having one's interest and attention inward or to things within oneself. Page 73.

in turn: one thing coming after another; in the proper order or sequence. Page 55.

in valence: being in one's own valence, one's actual personality. Page 116.

invalidate: deprive something or someone of its (their) force, value or effectiveness; make less of or nothing of. Page 84.

inventory: a step taken on a case, where information is gathered, such as name, age, height, weight, as well as information about past treatments, psychosomatic illnesses, operations and early environment. Page 152.

invertebrate: of or concerning any animal without a backbone or spinal column made of interlocking, flexible units (usually of bone called vertebrae). Invertebrates include jellyfish, worms, oysters, snails, etc. The *invertebrate stage* (chapter *Effort Processing*) would be that period of time in the evolutionary line when life forms had not yet developed backbones. Page 21.

inviolate: kept sacred (regarded with reverence and respect); free from disturbance or interference. Page 31.

is such that: of a degree, quality, condition, etc., as specified by the statement following, as in *"The co-existent relationship between Affinity, Reality and Communication is such that none can be increased without increasing the other two and none can be decreased without decreasing the other two."* Page 193.

jar: to bump or cause to move or shake from impact. Hence, to startle or unsettle; shock. Page 114.

kept in mind: carried in the mind; remembered, as of a fact or piece of information that is important or could be useful in the future. Page 14.

keys: vital or crucial elements. Page 14.

latent: coming after the fact of; present or existing but not developed, yet capable of being activated. Page 185.

lay bare: expose to view, reveal. Page 14.

legion: a very large number (as of persons or things). From its original meaning of a large division of the Roman army consisting of from 3,000 to 6,000 men. Page 153.

let go: to relax or release one's grasp or hold of. Used figuratively. Page 48.

lies: is found; consists or is based on (usually followed by *in*), as in *"The key to the processes outlined in this book lies in the SELF-DETERMINISM of individuals."* Page 7.

Life: the cause or source of living; the animating principle; soul. Page 47.

Life Static: see the Axioms in the chapter *Definitions, Logics and Axioms*. Page 129.

lift: become freer of aberrative influence. Page 69.

light, come to: to become known. Page 54.

line of protoplasm: the evolution of organisms themselves, continuing along a protoplasmic line from generation to generation. *Protoplasm* is the colorless, jelly-like liquid that is present in the cells of all living plants, animals and humans and consists of the living matter of plant and animal cells. Page 155.

listless: lacking energy or disinclined to exert effort; having or showing little or no interest in anything. Page 57.

literalness: the quality or state of being *literal,* taking words in their usual or most basic sense without interpretation or reason. A phrase in an engram means exactly what it says. Page 27.

lived only once theory: the unproven theory, based on the materialistic principle all is matter and there is nothing else, that a person lives only once without any prior existence and that there is no future beyond death. Page 58.

lock: an analytical moment in which the perceptics of an engram are approximated, thus restimulating the engram or bringing it into action, the present time perceptics being erroneously interpreted by the reactive mind to mean that the same condition which produced physical pain once before is now again at hand. Page 28.

locking: forming a lock. Page 105.

Lock Running: the action of processing and taking out a single lock by having an individual start in at the beginning of an incident and go on through, several times, running the lock just as one would an engram. Page 55.

LOCK SCANNING: A PROCESS WHICH STARTS THE PRECLEAR FROM A POINT IN THE PAST, WITH WHICH HE HAS MADE SOLID CONTACT, UP THROUGH ALL SIMILAR INCIDENTS, WITHOUT VERBALIZATION. THIS IS DONE OVER AND OVER, EACH TIME TRYING TO START AT AN EARLIER INCIDENT OF THE SAME KIND, UNTIL THE PRECLEAR EXTROVERTS ON THE SUBJECT OF THE CHAIN. "BOIL-OFF" OFTEN RESULTS, WHEREIN THE PRECLEAR SEEMS TO GO TO SLEEP. AVOID BOIL-OFF, FOR IT IS NOT THERAPEUTIC AND WILL EVENTUALLY RESULT IN REDUCED TONE. BOIL-OFF IS A LAZY AUDITOR'S EXCUSE TO BE IDLE AND FACSIMILES ARE IN SUCH SEVERE CONFLICT THAT THEY WILL NOT RESOLVE WITHOUT RESOLVING POSTULATES FIRST. LOCK SCANNING IS A STANDARDIZED DRILL, STARTED ON SIGNAL AND ENDED WITH THE PRECLEAR SAYING HE IS AGAIN IN PRESENT TIME. IT CAN BE DONE ON ANY SUBJECT. *ABOVE* 2.0 ONLY. (From *LRH Glossary*.) Page 28.

---

long line, the: a reference to the lengthy track of time through which a person has lived. Page 58.

long since: in the distant past; long ago. Page 148.

low-scale: pertaining to the condition of being low on the Tone Scale. Page 13.

low-toned: pertaining to the condition of being low on the Tone Scale. Page 8.

magnitude: 1. greatness in size or extent; greatness in significance or influence. Page 136.

2. relative size, amount, importance, extent or influence. Page 140.

magnitude, comparable: *comparable* means capable of being compared; having features in common with something else to permit or suggest comparison. *Magnitude* means relative size, amount, importance, extent or influence. A datum can be evaluated only by a datum of comparable magnitude. Page 163.

main, in the: in most cases; generally; usually. Page 122.

malformations: faults and departures from the normal shape, form or structure in a part of the body. Page 153.

Man: the human race or species, humankind, Mankind. Page 7.

man: a human being, without regard to sex or age; a person. Page 84.

marked: clearly defined and evident; noticeable. Page 7.

martyrdom: state of being a *martyr,* one who chooses to suffer death rather than renounce religious principles; one who makes great sacrifices or suffers much in order to further a belief, cause or principle. Page 121.

matter, no: it is of no consequence or importance; it makes no difference; regardless of. Page 22.

maximal: the highest or greatest possible. Page 184.

mechanical (practicality): of or pertaining to machines or the design, construction and use of machinery. Hence, *"of the highest mechanical practicality"* would mean as level-headedly and matter-of-factly demonstrable as that of the workability and operation of machines or their parts. Page 27.

mechanical (processes): involving or employing mechanical action, such as a series of specific procedures or steps taken to achieve a predictable result. Page 40.

mechanically: in a manner pertaining to a *mechanism,* the agency or means by which a phenomenon or effect is shown, evidenced or produced and likened to the structure or system of parts in a mechanical device for carrying out some function or doing something. Page 44.

mechanism: 1. a structure or system (of parts, components, etc.) that together perform a particular function as would occur in a machine. Page 10.

2. the agency or means by which an effect is produced or a purpose is accomplished, likened to the structure or system of parts in a mechanical device for carrying out some function or doing something. Page 80.

medicine: the medical profession. Page 166.

MEST: A COMPOUND WORD MADE UP OF THE FIRST LETTERS OF *MATTER, ENERGY, SPACE* AND *TIME.* A COINED WORD FOR THE *PHYSICAL UNIVERSE. THETA IS NOT CONSIDERED AS PART OF THE PHYSICAL UNIVERSE, BUT IS NOT CONSIDERED ABSOLUTELY AS NOT PART OF THE PHYSICAL UNIVERSE.* (From *LRH Glossary.*) Page 21.

MEST Processing: processing which calls for physical manifestation rather than words. MEST Processing reaches into that strata underlying language and processes the individual in the physical universe. It processes his communication lines directed toward matter, energy, space and time. For example, one could begin by asking for a time when the preclear had an object taken away from him; we are interested in the actual departure of the object, not in the words which accompany the departure. Page 101.

---

millennia: the plural form of *millennium,* a period of 1,000 years. Page 120.

mimicry: imitating the actions of another. For example, a person claps their hands, you clap your hands. All of a sudden the fellow recognizes there is something in his vicinity that is similar to him. Page 139.

mind, kept in: carried in the mind; remembered, as of a fact or piece of information that is important or could be useful in the future. Page 14.

–270°C: a reference to *absolute zero,* the temperature of –273.16°C, the point at which all molecular activity is thought to cease. Page 121.

mis-emotion: 1. *mis-* means mistaken, wrong, incorrect; thus mis-emotion is any emotion that is irrational or inappropriate to the present time environment. Page 9.
2. *mis-* abbreviation of *miserable, misery,* hence miserable emotion, such as Anger, Fear, Grief and Apathy. Page 130.

molecules: one of the basic units of matter, consisting of one or more atoms held together by chemical forces. They are the smallest particles into which a substance can be divided and still have the chemical identity of the original substance. Page 182.

monitor: regulate or control (some situation, process, operation, etc.). Page 43.

monocell: an organism composed of a single cell. A *cell* is the smallest structural unit of an organism that is capable of independent functioning. Page 21.

motor: of, pertaining to or involving muscular movement. Page 55.

motor control panels: a control and monitoring system the mind uses to direct the body. Thoughts register on the motor control panels which then cause the body to go into action. Page 55.

Move (Straightwire): a reference to a type of Straightwire command containing movement such as, "Can you recall a time when you moved an object" or "Can you recall a time when you were proud to move something heavy." Page 29.

muscular tension: the degree that a person's muscles are stretched, stressed, firm, stiff or contracted. Page 27.

myopia: a common condition of the eye in which distant objects cannot be seen sharply. Page 153.

mystic: 1. of obscure or vague character or significance; pertaining to mysterious qualities. Page 27.
2. a person who claims to attain, or believes in the possibility of attaining, insight into mysteries that go beyond ordinary human knowledge, as by direct communication with the spiritual or divine. Page 120.

native: belonging to, or connected with, a person or thing by nature, in contrast to what is acquired or added. Page 13.

native state: an original, pure (uncombined with other things), untouched form or condition. Page 7.

natural selection: the process by which forms of life having traits that better enable them to adapt to specific environmental pressures, such as predators, changes in climate, competition for food or mates, will tend to survive and reproduce in greater numbers than others of their kind, thus ensuring the perpetuation of those favorable traits in succeeding generations. Page 129.

necessity level: the degree of emergency in present time environment. It would be that amount of urgency or commotion necessary in the environment to extrovert the individual and put him into motion in present time. Page 39.

negative proof: evidence sufficient to establish a thing as true or produce belief in its truth, where the evidence is in the form of something that is omitted or absent. For example, "nobody was ill after eating the meal is *negative proof* that the food was not spoiled." Page 122.

Newton's laws: three laws formulated by English scientist and mathematician Sir Isaac Newton (1642–1727): (1) a body at rest remains at rest and a body in motion remains in motion unless acted on by an external force; (2) the motion of a body changes in proportion to the size of the force applied to it; (3) every action produces an equal but opposite reaction. Page 59.

Nirvana: the goal of the Hindus. Hindu beliefs are that "Reality is One" and that ultimate salvation, and release from the endless cycle of birth to death, is achieved when one merges or is absorbed back into the "one divine reality," with all loss of individual existence. Page 122.

no matter: it is of no consequence or importance; it makes no difference; regardless of. Page 22.

non-com: abbreviation for *non-commissioned officer,* a junior officer in a branch of the armed services. (A *commission* is the granting of authority to military officers issued by the president of the United States.) Page 115.

not being in body: a reference to a mystic practice in which the person sits immobile and in great concentration, letting himself drift towards the edge of utter relaxation. He is practicing an abandonment and death of the body. Page 121.

Not-Beingness: the state of being an effect, being effected by some exterior cause. Page 39.

notwithstanding: in spite of; regardless of. Page 129.

obtains: exists; establishes; has a place. Page 183.

occasion: bring about; cause. Page 14.

occluded: affected by *occlusion,* i.e., having memories shut off from one's awareness; from *occlude,* to close, shut or stop up (a passage, opening, etc.). Page 3.

of course: in the natural or expected order of things; naturally. Also with the sense of without any doubt; certainly. Page 55.

olfactory: of or pertaining to the sense of smell. Page 157.

-ology(ies): study or knowledge, usually in reference to any science or branch of knowledge; for example, biology (study of living organisms), geology (study of the physical history of Earth) or ethnology (study of the races of humankind). Page 22.

on the order of: resembling to some extent; like. Page 49.

on the part of: regarding or with respect to the person or thing that is specified. Page 8.

open (a case): to get (something or someone) going; to begin the operation of. Page 57.

optic nerve(s): the nerve that carries signals from the eye to the brain. *Optic* means of or relating to the eye or vision. Page 157.

order: an action, class, group or kind having rank in a scale of quality or importance, distinguished from others by nature or character. Page 27.

order of, on the: resembling to some extent; like. Page 49.

order of the day: the prevailing rule or custom of the time. Page 120.

organic: relating to or derived from living matter or materials. Page 22.

organically: in relation to bodily organs or their functions; in the manner of an organized living being. Page 21.

organism(s): a living thing, such as a plant, animal or bacteria; specifically, any individual animal or plant having various organs and parts that function together as a whole to maintain life and its activities. (An *organ* is a part of an organism, such as an eye, a wing or a leaf, that performs a specific function.) Page 21.

original cell: a reference to the theory that life forms began in a primitive ocean when supposedly spontaneous events created a single cell capable of reproducing other cells and hence, life forms. Page 122.

out of evidence: not visible, present or conspicuous. Page 30.

out of valence: the taking on of the physical and/or emotional characteristics or traits of another. Page 59.

overt action: any action whereby the individual hurts an entity on any one of the dynamics. Page 44.

pains, to take: to make efforts, accompanied with care and attention, to achieve a good or satisfactory result. Page 100.

paralleled: equaled or matched. A *parallel* in this sense is something identical or similar in essential respects to something else; match. Page 27.

parity: the state or condition of being equal, or on a level; equality. Page 25.

parlance: a particular manner or way of speaking; speech. Page 153.

particular: separate and distinct characteristics, qualities, etc., from others of the same group, category or nature; of or belonging to a single, definite thing; not general. Page 53.

particular, in: especially or specifically. Page 29.

part of, on the: regarding or with respect to the person or thing that is specified. Page 8.

PAST POSTULATES: DECISIONS OR CONCLUSIONS THE PRECLEAR HAS MADE IN THE PAST AND TO WHICH HE IS STILL SUBJECTED IN THE PRESENT. PAST POSTULATES ARE UNIFORMLY INVALID SINCE THEY CANNOT RESOLVE PRESENT ENVIRONMENT. (From *LRH Glossary*.) Page 26.

patter: speech or words associated with a particular situation, profession or group of persons. Page 100.

peculiarity: a feature or trait that is uniquely characteristic of a particular thing. Page 44.

perceptics: perceived and recorded sense messages, such as smell, taste, touch, sound, sight, etc. Page 49.

PERCEPTIONS: BY MEANS OF PHYSICAL WAVES, RAYS AND PARTICLES OF THE PHYSICAL UNIVERSE, IMPRESSIONS OF THE ENVIRONMENT ENTER THROUGH THE "SENSE CHANNELS," SUCH AS THE EYES AND OPTIC NERVES, THE NOSE AND OLFACTORY NERVES, THE EARS AND AURAL NERVES, INTERBODY NERVES

FOR INTERBODY PERCEPTIONS, ETC., ETC. THESE ARE ALL "PERCEPTIONS" UP TO THE INSTANT THEY RECORD AS FACSIMILES, AT WHICH MOMENT THEY BECOME "RECORDINGS." WHEN RECALLED THEY ARE PERCEPTIONS AGAIN, BEING AGAIN ENTERED INTO SENSE CHANNELS FROM THE RECALL SIDE. THERE ARE OVER HALF A HUNDRED SEPARATE PERCEPTIONS ALL BEING RECORDED AT ONCE. (From *LRH Glossary*.) Page 30.

phenomena: occurrences, circumstances or facts that are perceptible by the senses, and sometimes viewed as significant or in need of explanation. Page 21.

photon: of a *photon,* a unit particle of light. Just as matter is composed of atoms, light is composed of photons. Page 58.

photon converters: organisms such as algae and plankton that convert units of light (photons) from the Sun and minerals from the sea into energy they need to survive. Page 58.

physiological: of the functions and activities of a living, material organism and its parts, including all its physical and chemical processes. Page 146.

physique: physical or bodily structure, appearance or muscular development. Page 186.

pick(ing) up: figuratively, take hold of and raise something up so as to examine, use, recover, etc. Page 10.

plastically: in a manner like that of plastic, that is, able to be impressed upon, shaped or molded. Page 188.

play, called into: caused or put into operation; caused to come into force or activity. Page 13.

plotted: laid out or shown the process, condition or course of something, as if with the precision used to chart the course of a ship, draw a map of an area, etc. Page 180.

plus: having a certain quantity added to what is already being referred to. Page 179.

poliomyelitis: a highly infectious disease, widespread in the 1950s, that usually occurred in children and young adults. It affected the brain and spinal cord, sometimes leading to a loss of voluntary movement and muscular wasting (loss of muscular strength or substance). Page 153.

poses: presents; amounts to. Page 129.

posing: 1. assuming a certain attitude. Page 44.
2. putting forward or setting forth (a question, problem, etc.). Page 106.

positive proof: evidence sufficient to establish a thing as true or produce belief in its truth, where such evidence does not admit any question and is stated as something explicit, express, definite, precise and emphatic. For example, "he won the race which is *positive proof* that he was the fastest runner that day." Page 122.

POSTULATE: *(NOUN)* A CONCLUSION, DECISION OR RESOLUTION MADE BY THE INDIVIDUAL HIMSELF ON HIS OWN SELF-DETERMINISM ON DATA OF THE PAST, KNOWN OR UNKNOWN. THE POSTULATE IS ALWAYS KNOWN. IT IS MADE UPON THE EVALUATION OF DATA BY THE INDIVIDUAL OR ON IMPULSE WITHOUT DATA. IT RESOLVES A PROBLEM OF THE PAST, DECIDES ON PROBLEMS OR OBSERVATIONS IN THE PRESENT OR SETS A PATTERN FOR THE FUTURE. (From *LRH Glossary.*) Page 8.

POSTULATE: *(VERB)* TO CONCLUDE, DECIDE OR RESOLVE A PROBLEM OR TO SET A PATTERN FOR THE FUTURE OR TO NULLIFY A PATTERN OF THE PAST. (From *LRH Glossary.*) Page 9.

postulations: assumptions, especially as a basis for reasoning. Page 73.

practicality: that which stresses workability or effectiveness as tested by actual experience; unspeculative; matter-of-fact. Page 27.

PRECLEAR: ONE WHO HAS ENTERED PROCESSING EN ROUTE TO BECOMING A FIFTEEN. *See also* **FIFTEEN.** (From *LRH Glossary.*) Page 3.

present time problems: present time problems are fully described in the chapter *Present Time Problems*. Page 3.

Prime Static: *prime* means basic or fundamental. *Static* is that which is without wavelength, weight, mass or position in space. See the Axioms in the chapter *Definitions, Logics and Axioms*. Page 39.

processed out: been removed or made ineffective by the application of auditing techniques. Page 48.

propitiation: a low emotion below Anger and close to Apathy. *Propitiation* is the act of trying to please or satisfy someone in a way calculated to win their favor in order to defend or protect oneself against their disapproval, attack, etc. Page 120.

protagonist: the leading or principal figure in a situation or course of events. A *protagonist* is the main character in a drama or other literary work and is often contrasted with the *antagonist,* the principal character in opposition (such as a villain) to the main character or hero (protagonist) of a narrative or drama. Page 21.

protoplasm: the colorless, jelly-like liquid that is present in the cells of all living plants, animals and humans and consists of the living matter of plant and animal cells. From German *protoplasma*, literally, first created thing. Page 155.

protoplasm line: the evolution of organisms themselves, continuing along a protoplasmic line from generation to generation. *Protoplasm* is the colorless, jelly-like liquid that is present in the cells of all living plants, animals and humans and consists of the living matter of plant and animal cells. Page 155.

pseudo-: a word combined with other words to mean false or pretended. Also, apparently similar to (a specified thing). Page 150.

psychosomatic: *see* PSYCHOSOMATIC ILLNESS.

PSYCHOSOMATIC ILLNESS: A TERM USED IN COMMON PARLANCE TO DENOTE A CONDITION "RESULTING FROM A STATE OF MIND." SUCH ILLNESSES ACCOUNT FOR ABOUT 70 PERCENT OF ALL ILLS, BY POPULAR REPORT. TECHNICALLY, IN THIS SCIENCE,

"A CHRONIC OR CONTINUING PAINFUL FACSIMILE TO WHICH THE PRECLEAR IS HOLDING TO ACCOUNT FOR FAILURES." ARTHRITIS, BURSITIS, TENDONITIS, MYOPIA, ASTIGMATISM, BIZARRE ACHES AND PAINS, SINUSITIS, COLDS, ULCERS, MIGRAINE HEADACHES, TOOTHACHE, POLIOMYELITIS DEFORMITIES, FATNESS, SKIN MALFORMATIONS, ETC., ETC., ETC., ETC., ARE A FEW OF THESE LEGION OF CHRONIC SOMATICS. THEY ARE TRACEABLE TO SERVICE FACSIMILES. (From *LRH Glossary*.) Page 10.

PSYCHOTIC: AN INDIVIDUAL WHO IS OUT OF CONTACT TO A THOROUGH EXTENT WITH HIS PRESENT TIME ENVIRONMENT AND WHO DOES NOT COMPUTE INTO THE FUTURE. HE MAY BE AN ACUTE PSYCHOTIC, WHEREIN HE BECOMES PSYCHOTIC FOR ONLY A FEW MINUTES AT A TIME AND ONLY OCCASIONALLY IN CERTAIN ENVIRONMENTS (AS IN RAGES OR APATHIES), OR HE MAY BE A CHRONIC PSYCHOTIC (OR IN A CONTINUAL DISCONNECT WITH THE FUTURE AND PRESENT). PSYCHOTICS WHO ARE DRAMATICALLY HARMFUL TO OTHERS ARE CONSIDERED DANGEROUS ENOUGH TO BE PUT AWAY. PSYCHOTICS WHO ARE HARMFUL ON A LESS DRAMATIC BASIS ARE NO LESS HARMFUL TO THEIR ENVIRONMENT AND ARE NO LESS PSYCHOTIC. (From *LRH Glossary*.) Page 26.

punitive: involving or intending to inflict punishment, so as to have a preventive, restraining or limiting effect on something. Page 56.

puppet-like: like a puppet, a movable model or figure of a person, typically manipulated by a puppet master through strings or wires. Hence, a *puppet* is a person whose actions, ideas, etc., are controlled by someone or something else. Page 75.

purveyor: one who provides, supplies or furnishes something. Page 14.

put away: place someone into a mental institution. Page 150.

randomity: see Axioms 69 and 73 in the chapter *Definitions, Logics and Axioms*. Page 110.

rarity: relative fewness in number; the fact of being or occurring seldom or in few instances; an uncommon occurrence. Page 121.

rays, cosmic: electrically charged, high-energy particles of great penetrating power, that travel through space, such as those emitted from an exploding sun or star, and which reach the Earth. *Cosmic* means of or relating to the universe, especially as distinct from Earth. Page 21.

reaction time: the amount of time it takes someone to react to or do something in the environment (or during a test), such as making a decision, solving a problem, grabbing something dropped, etc. Page 27.

record: a reference to a *phonograph record,* a 12-inch disc with grooves on which music is recorded so it can be played over and over. Page 91.

RECOVERY: RECOVERY OF ONE'S OWN ABILITY TO DETERMINE ONE'S EXISTENCE. (From *LRH Glossary.*) Page 27.

relay system: a functioning related group of elements or parts that pass along (relay) instructions, information, commands, impulses, etc. *Relay* means of or pertaining to a station or unit that receives and passes on information. A *system* is an organized group of elements functioning as one unit. Page 152.

RELEASE: *(VERB)* THE ACT OF TAKING THE PERCEPTIONS OR EFFORT OR EFFECTIVENESS OUT OF A HEAVY FACSIMILE, OR TAKING AWAY THE PRECLEAR'S HOLD ON THE FACSIMILE. (From *LRH Glossary.*) Page 28.

Repeater Technique: the repetition of a word or phrase in order to produce movement on the time track into an entheta area containing that word or phrase. Page 57.

repertoire: the stock of plays, operas, roles, songs, etc., that a company, actor, singer, etc., is familiar with and can perform. Used figuratively. Page 154.

REPETITIVE STRAIGHTWIRE: ATTENTION CALLED TO AN INCIDENT OVER AND OVER, AMONGST OTHER INCIDENTS, UNTIL IT IS DESENSITIZED. USED ON CONCLUSIONS OR INCIDENTS WHICH DO NOT EASILY SURRENDER. (From *LRH Glossary*.) Page 28.

run: audit or process; apply a process or processes to someone. Page 10.

rung: a stage or degree in a scale. Literally, a *rung* is a sturdy stick, bar or rod, often a rounded one, used as one of the steps of a ladder. Page 132.

running: auditing or processing; applying a process or processes to someone. Page 9.

running back: finding or discovering something (such as tracing down a sequence of development, origin, cause, etc.) by careful search. Page 65.

running on: functioning, operating or working. Page 28.

running out: exhausting the negative influence of something; erasing. Page 29.

scale: short for *Tone Scale,* a scale of emotional tones which shows the levels of human behavior. These tones, ranged from the highest to the lowest, are, in part, Enthusiasm, Boredom, Antagonism, Anger, Covert Hostility, Fear, Grief and Apathy. Page 3.

scan: the action of Lock Scanning. Page 136.

scanned: given Lock Scanning. Page 76.

scanned off: glanced over systematically until it is no longer affecting the individual. (*Off* means so as to no longer be attached or connected; eliminate or remove something.) Page 57.

science: knowledge; comprehension or understanding of facts or principles, classified and made available in work, life or the search for truth. A science is a connected body of demonstrated truths or observed facts systematically organized and bound together under general laws. It includes trustworthy methods for the discovery of new truth within its domain and denotes the application of scientific methods in fields of study previously considered open only to theories based on subjective, historical or undemonstrable, abstract criteria. The word *science* is used in this sense—the most fundamental meaning and tradition of the word—and not in the sense of the *physical* or *material* sciences. Page 17.

scouted: searched for something; explored or examined. Page 80.

secondaries: moments of acute loss as death of a loved one. The subject of secondaries and their processing is contained in *Science of Survival*. Page 44.

Selective Service: *Selective Service System,* an independent agency of the United States government whose purpose is to provide men required by law to serve in the military. Page 130.

self-auditing: the action of a preclear attempting to audit himself. Self-auditing is normally done out of valence. Self-auditing is not the same as *self-processing,* the action of the preclear using the *Handbook for Preclears* without an auditor. Page 60.

self-determinism: that state of being wherein the individual can or cannot be controlled by his environment according to his own choice. Page 7.

Self-determinism Processing: processing which restores basic self-determinism to the preclear. In Self-determinism Processing, the individual contacts his own decisions to be aberrated and comes to understand that he is aberrated by his own choice. The objective in this type of processing is to give the preclear back to himself. Page 9.

self-help book: a reference to *Handbook for Preclears,* the companion book to *Advanced Procedure and Axioms.* Page 141.

SERVICE FACSIMILE: A DEFINITELY NON-SURVIVAL SITUATION CONTAINED IN A FACSIMILE WHICH IS CALLED INTO ACTION BY THE INDIVIDUAL TO EXPLAIN HIS FAILURES. A SERVICE FACSIMILE MAY BE ONE OF AN ILLNESS, AN INJURY, AN INABILITY. THE FACSIMILE BEGINS WITH A DOWN EMOTIONAL CURVE AND ENDS WITH AN UPWARD EMOTIONAL CURVE. BETWEEN THESE

IT HAS PAIN. A SERVICE FACSIMILE *IS* THE PATTERN WHICH IS THE CHRONIC "PSYCHOSOMATIC ILLNESS." IT MAY CONTAIN COUGHS, FEVER, ACHES, RASHES, ANY MANIFESTATION OF A NON-SURVIVAL CHARACTER, MENTAL OR PHYSICAL. IT MAY EVEN BE A SUICIDE EFFORT. IT IS COMPLETE WITH ALL PERCEPTIONS. IT HAS MANY SIMILAR FACSIMILES. IT HAS MANY LOCKS. THE POSSESSION AND USE OF A SERVICE FACSIMILE DISTINGUISHES A HOMO SAPIENS. A SERVICE FACSIMILE IS THAT FACSIMILE WHICH THE PRECLEAR USES TO APOLOGIZE FOR HIS FAILURES. IN OTHER WORDS, IT IS USED TO MAKE OTHERS WRONG AND PROCURE THEIR COOPERATION IN THE SURVIVAL OF THE PRECLEAR. (From *LRH Glossary.*) Page 3.

SERVICE FACSIMILE CHAIN: THE ENTIRE CHAIN OF SIMILAR INCIDENTS WHICH COMPRISE THE TOTAL REPERTOIRE OF THE INDIVIDUAL WHO IS EXPLAINING HIS FAILURE AND THUS SEEKING SUPPORT. (From *LRH Glossary.*) Page 28.

servomechanism: a mechanism that serves, services or aids something. Specifically, the human mind is a servomechanism to all mathematics because mathematics is something which Man uses to solve problems: without the human mind mathematics is of no use. Page 166.

session: a period of time given to or set aside for the pursuit of a particular activity. Specifically, it refers to a period of time set aside for *processing,* the application of a set of exact verbal procedures and exercises which raise tone and increase perception and memory. Page 26.

set in their ways: of persons who have long-established habits or opinions and are unlikely or reluctant to change. Page 63.

severely: in a manner that is harsh, extreme, unpleasantly violent or causes discomfort by extreme character or conditions, as weather, cold, heat or wind. Page 21.

shellfish: an animal living in water, that has a soft body, a hard outer covering or shell but no backbone, and that may be eaten as food. Shellfish include the mollusks, such as oysters and clams, and the crustaceans, such as shrimps, crabs and lobsters. Shellfish marked a stage of the evolutionary line from the complicated but still microscopic monocell which developed into vegetable matter, became jellyfish, then became a mollusk and made its transition into crustaceans. Page 58.

short, in: introducing a summary statement in a few words of what has been previously stated; in summary. Page 28.

short of: without going to the point of or so far as. Page 13.

shuddered away: drawn away from something out of fear or disgust, as if shivering or shaking from such. Page 110.

shunt: shove or push (something) aside often to an alternate course; evade. Page 128.

sick: suffering from or affected with a physical illness. Page 109.

signal: remarkable, notable or outstanding, as in *"several signal successes."* Page 18.

signal, started on: begun upon the receipt of a known sign or event, likened to the use of a gun in the starting of a race, where participants start running as soon as they hear the sound of the gun being fired. *Signal* means anything that serves to indicate, direct or command. Page 154.

sinusitis: inflammation of a sinus or the sinuses (the spaces in the bone behind a person's nose which serve to lighten the head and cushion the brain from blows to the front of the skull). Page 153.

sociology: the study of the origin, development and structure of human societies and the behavior of individuals and groups in them. Page 166.

somatic: the word *somatic* is used to denote physical pain or discomfort of any kind. It can mean actual pain, such as that caused by a cut or a blow; or it can mean discomfort, as from heat or cold; it can mean itching—in short, anything physically uncomfortable. It is a non-survival physical state of being. Page 30.

species: a group or class of animals or plants having certain common and permanent characteristics which clearly distinguish it from other groups and which can breed with one another. Page 122.

speculations: conclusions, opinions, reasons, etc. Also, contemplation or consideration of a subject as well as the conclusion(s) reached from that. Page 162.

spindly: having a slender, elongated form implying weakness. Page 121.

spring (from): to originate or arise from a specific source or cause; to come forth or come into being from, likened to a spring that moves suddenly or rapidly upwards. Page 63.

started on signal: begun upon the receipt of a known sign or event, likened to the use of a gun in the starting of a race, where participants start running as soon as they hear the sound of the gun being fired. *Signal* means anything that serves to indicate, direct or command. Page 154.

Start, Stop, Change Straightwire: a reference to a type of Straightwire command containing either start, stop or change. For instance, "Can you recall a time when you started a machine" or "Can you recall an incident when you stopped somebody from being terrified" or "Can you recall a time when you changed something for the better." These forms of Straightwire can be found in *Self Analysis* which is based on the formula of control: start, stop and change. Page 140.

static: 1. a thing of no motion. It is a causative static. A true static does not have wavelength so it is not in motion. It does not have weight, it does not have mass, it does not have length nor breadth. It is motionlessness. See the Axioms in the chapter *Definitions, Logics and Axioms.* Page 39.
2. fixed; stable. Page 79.

stimuli: plural of *stimulus,* any action or agent that causes or changes an activity in an organism, organ or part, as something that starts a nerve impulse, activates a muscle, etc. Page 59.

stimulus-response: a certain stimulus (something that rouses a person or thing to activity or energy or that produces a reaction in the body) automatically giving a certain response. Page 10.

stirs: causes to be emotionally moved or strongly affected by; excites. Page 128.

Stop, Start, Change Straightwire: a reference to a type of Straightwire command containing either start, stop or change. For instance, "Can you recall a time when you started a machine" or "Can you recall an incident when you stopped somebody from being terrified" or "Can you recall a time when you changed something for the better." These forms of Straightwire can be found in *Self Analysis* which is based on the formula of control: start, stop and change. Page 29.

store, in: put away, keep or accumulate in a separate place, as if for future use. Page 47.

STRAIGHTWIRE: A PROCESS OF RECALLING FROM PRESENT TIME, WITH SOME PERCEPTION OR AT LEAST A CONCEPT, A PAST INCIDENT. THE NAME STRAIGHTWIRE DERIVES FROM THE *MEST* COMMUNICATIONS PROCESS OF CONNECTING TWO POINTS OF A COMMUNICATIONS SYSTEM. IT IS ESSENTIALLY MEMORY WORK. IT IS APPLIED TO POSTULATES, EVALUATIONS, INCIDENTS, SCENES, EMOTIONS, OR ANY DATA WHICH MAY BE IN THE STORAGE BANKS OF THE MIND WITHOUT "SENDING THE PRECLEAR" INTO THE INCIDENT ITSELF. IT IS DONE WITH THE PRECLEAR SITTING UP, EYES OPEN OR SHUT. THE AUDITOR IS VERY ALERT. STRAIGHTWIRE IS DONE RAPIDLY. THE PRECLEAR IS NOT PERMITTED TO WANDER OR REMINISCE. HE RESPONDS TO QUESTIONS ON THE PART OF THE AUDITOR. *MANY PRECLEARS DISLIKE BEING QUESTIONED. THE AUDITOR MUST THEN FIRST*

RESOLVE THE POSTULATES AGAINST BEING QUESTIONED. THIS
WOULD BE CALLED "CLEARING FOR BROAD STRAIGHTWIRE."
(From *LRH Glossary.*) Page 28.

Straightwire: fully described in *Science of Survival* and *Self Analysis*.
Page 40.

Straightwire (oneself): a method of auditing self by remembering
specific things about oneself. Page 26.

sub-control center: *see* CENTER OF CONTROL.

subjected to: caused to undergo the action of something specified;
exposed (to). Page 9.

subservient: under the authority of something else; secondary to.
Page 146.

successively: in succession, following or happening one upon another.
Page 3.

sweeping (through): passing over or through a surface or substance
with a continuous movement. Page 153.

swing of, into a (better): getting used to a situation or activity and
taking an active or lively part in it. Page 100.

switchboard: a board containing switches and other devices for
controlling electric flows and used to connect and disconnect
communication lines. Used to describe the brain and nervous
and glandular system. Page 148.

SYMPATHY: THE POSING OF AN EMOTIONAL STATE SIMILAR TO
THE EMOTIONAL STATE OF AN INDIVIDUAL IN GRIEF OR APATHY.
(From *LRH Glossary.*) Page 3.

sympathy exciters: entities on any dynamic for which the individual
has felt sympathy of the variety between 0.9 and 0.4. See chapter
Sympathy Exciters. Page 3.

tamper with: interfere with something (so as to change). Page 83.

tapped the reservoirs of: to tap the reservoirs of something is to
draw from its material or resources. Page 30.

technician: an expert who is greatly skilled in the practical application of something, such as a specific process. Page 17.

TEN: A CASE ADVANCED TO THE POINT OF RELEASED SERVICE FACSIMILE. (From *LRH Glossary*.) Page 30.

tendonitis: inflammation of a *tendon,* an elastic cord or band of tough white tissue that attaches a muscle to a bone or other part of the body. Page 153.

tension, muscular: the degree that a person's muscles are stretched, stressed, firm, stiff or contracted. Page 27.

therapeutic: about, involving or used in the alleviation of mental or spiritual travail. Page 99.

thermal: of or pertaining to heat; measured, caused, operated or determined by heat. Page 170.

THETA: THE MATHEMATICAL SYMBOL—θ—FOR THE STATIC OF THOUGHT. BY THETA IS MEANT THE STATIC ITSELF. BY "FACSIMILE" IS MEANT THETA WHICH CONTAINS IMPRESSIONS BY PERCEPTION. (From *LRH Glossary*.) Page 9.

theta facsimile(s): a picture of the physical universe. It is not the actual thing, it is a memory recording. It is a number of perceptions all packaged up. *Facsimile* means something similar to. Page 39.

THOUGHT: THE FACSIMILES ONE HAS RECORDED OF HIS VARIOUS ENVIRONMENTS AND THE FACSIMILES HE HAS CREATED WITH HIS IMAGININGS, THEIR RECOMBINATION AND EVALUATIONS AND CONCLUSIONS, FOR THE PURPOSE OF DETERMINING ACTION OR NO ACTION OR POTENTIAL ACTION OR NO ACTION. THOUGHT IS USED ALSO TO MEAN A PROCESS TREATING AWARENESS LEVEL RECORDINGS, AS DISTINCT FROM NON-AWARENESS LEVEL RECORDINGS. (From *LRH Glossary*.) Page 3.

through all: in every point; in all respects. Page 129.

time track: the track of time through which a person has lived. Page 49.

tinged with: having a slight amount of some quality or characteristic. Page 27.

---

to date: until now. Page 22.

tolerance band: the range or level (as on a scale) in which something has the capacity to survive. Page 172.

tone: the momentary or continuing emotional state of the person. Page 3.

Tone Scale: a scale of emotional tones which shows the levels of human behavior. These tones, ranged from the highest to the lowest, are, in part, Enthusiasm, Boredom, Antagonism, Anger, Covert Hostility, Fear, Grief and Apathy. Page 3.

tonus: tone; state of tension or responsiveness. Page 28.

to the end (of): to the result or outcome; for the purpose. Page 25.

to this end: for this purpose; for this reason. Page 28.

touchable: able to be matched in quality, quantity, ability to do something, etc. Page 129.

track: short for *time track,* the track of time through which a person has lived. Page 48.

track: a distinct path along which something moves, evolves or develops; a course of action. Page 128.

trail blazed: marked out a path or route; to have set an example by being the first to do something; pioneered. *Blazed* here literally means marked with *blazes,* marks made on a tree by cutting the bark so as to mark a route *(trail).* Page 58.

travail: mental (or bodily) pain or suffering. Page 100.

tricks: acts involving or requiring skill and effectiveness. Page 58.

trigger mechanism: literally, a *trigger* is a device that releases a spring or similar item that sets off something else. A *mechanism* is a physical device for doing something. Hence, a *trigger mechanism* is a thing that acts to set off or put into action something else. Page 54.

tripped into: caused to fall into (something unpleasant). Used figuratively. Page 44.

tritely and truly: used in reference to a phrase or statement that, although often repeated, nevertheless holds true. *Tritely* means constantly stated or repeated to a point of being commonly known. Page 18.

turn, in: one thing coming after another; in the proper order or sequence. Page 55.

turn(s) on: start operating as if by means of a switch or button; activate. Page 57.

–270°C: a reference to *absolute zero,* the temperature of –273.16°C, the point at which all molecular activity is thought to cease. Page 121.

ulcers: open sores (other than a wound) on the skin or some internal organ, as the lining of the stomach, characterized by the disintegration of the affected tissue. Page 153.

unwarranted: not agreed upon; without approval. Page 188.

valence(s): literally, the word means the ability to combine with or take on parts of another. In its specialized meaning, *valence* is an actual or shadow personality. Being *out of valence* is the taking on of the physical and/or emotional characteristics or traits of another. *In valence* means being in one's own valence, one's actual personality. Page 59.

valence, in: being in one's own valence, one's actual personality. Page 116.

valence, out of: the taking on of the physical and/or emotional characteristics or traits of another. Page 59.

Valhalla: in Norse mythology, the hall of Odin (king of the gods) where the souls of heroes slain in battle and others who died bravely are received. Page 122.

Validation MEST: Validation MEST Processing, processing that orients the individual to the present time and the physical universe—matter, energy, space and time—MEST. The concentration is on the analytical moments of any given incident, as opposed to the painful moments. Page 139.

---

vectors: things which have both direction and quantity. For example, force would be a vector as it has a direction and an amount but mass is not a vector as it has no direction. Page 179.

vertebrate: of or concerning any animal with a backbone or spinal column, made of interlocking, flexible units (usually of bone called vertebrae). Vertebrates include fish, reptiles, as well as birds and mammals. The *vertebrate stage* would be that period of time in the evolutionary line when life forms developed backbones. Page 58.

virus: a minute organism that lives as a parasite in plants, animals and bacteria and can only multiply within living cells and not independently. Page 174.

visios: visible recalls; for example, recalling a scene by seeing it again. Page 135.

vital: full of life. Page 40.

wavelength: a wavelength is the distance from the crest to crest of a wave. The relative distance from crest to crest in any flow of energy. Page 148.

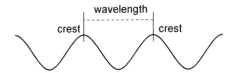

wherein: in what or in which (place, thing, condition, matter, action, etc.); in, at, during or in the course of which. Page 18.

which is to say: a phrase used to introduce a clearer, more comprehensible, restatement of what immediately precedes or to limit or modify it. Page 53.

wide-open: *wide-open* is defined in the chapter *Wide-Open and Occluded*. Page 3.

will, at: just as or when one wishes. Page 115.

wise: way or manner. Page 9.

wished (something) upon: desired or wanted something (unpleasant) to occur or happen to someone. Page 10.

wishing off (something upon someone): hoping to give or pass on something unwanted to someone. Page 14.

witness, as: used to introduce something that gives evidence of a fact or demonstrates a statement just made. Page 129.

words, in other: put differently; otherwise stated, often used to introduce an explanation of something and usually in a simpler way. Page 39.

worked: acted upon or influenced; acted on; specifically practiced (one's occupation or profession) on. Page 109.

worked upon: acted upon or influenced. Page 7.

wrong side of the board: meaning the disadvantageous, undesirable side of some place, object or situation, likened to a game played on a board such as that used for the game of chess. Page 49.

*I*NDEX

A

AAs, 13, 130

aberrated behavior

  description, 188

aberration, 180, 185, 192

  cycle of responsibility and, 128

  definition, 188

  self-determinism and, 8

  sources of, 55, 57

absolutes, 163

accessibility, 26

  broad techniques, 35

  definition, 150

  inaccessible "normal," 75

accusation, 131

  assuming "fault" and, 132

action definition, 163

action phrases, 175

Act(s), 145

  definition, 145

One to Fifteen

  described, 26–30

  summarized, 139–141

Adam, 122

Advanced Procedure, 25–31

  essence of, 31

  summary of, 139–141

aesthetic product

  definition, 193

affinity, 184

  definition, 184

age flashes, 139

alignment, 196

ally

  Death, 114

  locating, 44

ambition, 109

anesthesia, 79

anesthetic, 59

Anger, 29, 56, 130, 152

Antagonism, 56, 130, 152

  emotional curve, 114